ASHE Higher Education
Kelly Ward, Lisa E. Wolf-Wend

The Ecology of College Readiness

Karen D. Arnold

Elissa C. Lu

Kelli J. Armstrong

Discover this journal online at

WILEY ONLINE LIBRARY

wileyonlinelibrary.com

The Ecology of College Readiness
Karen D. Arnold, Elissa C. Lu, Kelli J. Armstrong
ASHE Higher Education Report: Volume 38, Number 5
Kelly Ward, Lisa E. Wolf-Wendel, Series Editors

Cover image by a_Taiga/©iStockphoto.

ISSN 1551-6970   electronic ISSN 1554-6306   ISBN 978-1-1185-5975-8

The ASHE Higher Education Report is part of the Jossey-Bass Higher and Adult Education Series and is published six times a year by Wiley Subscription Services, Inc., A Wiley Company, at Jossey-Bass, One Montgomery Street, Suite 1200, San Francisco, California 94104-4594.

Individual subscription rate (in USD): $174 per year US/Can/Mex, $210 rest of world; institutional subscription rate: $307 US, $367 Can/Mex, $418 rest of world. Single copy rate: $29. Electronic only–all regions: $174 individual, $307 institutional; Print & Electronic–US: $192 individual, $353 institutional; Print & Electronic–Canada/Mexico: $192 individual, $413 institutional; Print & Electronic– Rest of World: $228 individual, $464 institutional. See the Back Issue/Subscription Order Form in the back of this volume.

CALL FOR PROPOSALS: Prospective authors are strongly encouraged to contact Kelly Ward (kaward@wsu.edu) or Lisa Wolf-Wendel (lwolf@ku.edu). See "About the ASHE Higher Education Report Series" in the back of this volume.

Visit the Jossey-Bass Web site at **www.josseybass.com.**

The ASHE Higher Education Report is indexed in CIJE: Current Index to Journals in Education (ERIC), Education Index/Abstracts (H.W. Wilson), ERIC Database (Education Resources Information Center), Higher Education Abstracts (Claremont Graduate University), IBR & IBZ: International Bibliographies of Periodical Literature (K.G. Saur), and Resources in Education (ERIC).

Advisory Board

The ASHE Higher Education Report Series is sponsored by the Association for the Study of Higher Education (ASHE), which provides an editorial advisory board of ASHE members.

Contents

Executive Summary

Despite broad agreement that postsecondary education is increasingly necessary for individual and national well-being, there is a pronounced and widening socioeconomic gap in college access and success in the United States. The leading cause for this gap is a lack of college readiness: the multidimensional set of skills, traits, habits, and knowledge that students need to enter and succeed in college. Despite extensive research, policy, and practice efforts to improve college readiness, the problem has proven intractable because of the complexity of the interacting personal, organizational, and societal factors in play.

The human ecology theory of Urie Bronfenbrenner (1917–2005) addresses calls for an integrative framework that accounts for and offers new ways of looking at the complexity of college readiness. An ecological framework encompasses the interacting forces of ideology and culture, social and organizational structure, time, and individual agency. Furthermore, this framework provides an analytical tool to identify gaps in the existing literature and points to opportunities for research, policy, and practice.

Bronfenbrenner's ecology theory encompasses the many environments affecting students' college readiness. The ecology of the individual student determines whether that student leaves high school with the necessary constellation of aspirations, dispositions, and academic and practical knowledge. The key element of academic preparation, like all other readiness traits, is an outcome of developmentally instigative characteristics by which individuals choose, shape, and respond to environments such as school and college readiness programs.

Although embodied in individuals, college readiness is formed in microsystems, the immediate settings in which students experience everyday life in direct interaction with people, activities, roles, and objects. Classrooms, programs, families, friends, teachers, counselors, and extracurricular activities are examples of microsystems for students. Positive development occurs when individuals encounter increasing complexity within their immediate settings and relationships.

Higher education aspirations and college readiness are affected by the intersecting orbits in which students are simultaneously involved. The mesosystem consists of interactions of overlapping relationships, messages, objects, and symbols in students' immediate settings. Parental involvement in schools and dual enrollment in high school and college are examples of mesosytem interactions. The mesosystem is a crucial layer of the environment for college readiness because the totality of students' experience determines their educational dispositions and behaviors.

The structural arrangements of society and its institutions are designed and modified in a level of the environment where students are not present but that affects their lives. The exosystem level is the only place where systemic change and improvement can occur. The architects of the exosystem include the stakeholders who make policy, direct resources, design programs and interventions, and determine the criteria for entrance and success in educational institutions. This level of the environment sets the ground rules for the opportunities, experiences, and environments that students encounter and determines how organizations, programs, and educational interventions embody these possibilities.

At the broadest level of the ecology, the macrosystem, culture and ideology frame both the overall structure of schooling and the patterns of opportunities and perceived possibilities for different students. The macrosystem influences the ways dominant cultural and subcultural ideas and practices affect everything from policy to higher education costs and individual aspirations.

Finally, the chronosystem refers to temporal elements of environmental change, such as sequential college readiness tasks, chronological age and cohort, and developmental growth. The intersection of an individual life and sociohistorical context is a key determinant of educational outcomes.

As a developmental systems model, ecological theory provides a way of addressing college readiness by focusing on multiple, integrated interactions of people, organizations, systems, culture, and time. In this model, environments are more than interactive: they are mutually constituting. Students develop the aspirations and behaviors that affect their academic preparation in light of the opportunities, resources, and hazards that originate beyond their immediate environments. At the same time, students play an important role in shaping their experience through the ways in which they engage and respond to their environments.

The ecological model has several large implications for improving college readiness through research, policy, and practice. Most fundamental, the many stakeholders in the arena of college access and success need to understand that efforts to improve student readiness involve an ecological system. Researchers, policymakers, organizational leaders, and program designers must attend to the interactions of multiple environments and simultaneous interventions that affect the operation and evaluation of any initiative. Policies and programs need to account for the interconnections among the multiple settings and tasks involved in college access and success. Teachers, counselors, school leaders, and program staff must design activities and tasks that promote student engagement in experiences of increasing complexity. Practitioners also need to understand how students differ in making use of classrooms and program activities according to individuals' characteristic ways of engaging and responding to environments. No single policy, program, or intervention can influence all levels of a student's ecology. The ecological lens implies the need to coordinate efforts that affect students across the environment of their lives, promote consonance across divergent settings, and connect the elements of college readiness.

The systemic structures supporting and surrounding the educational environments of economically and educationally challenged students are not currently designed to sustain a comprehensive model such as the ecological approach. K–12 educational systems in the United States have evolved independently from higher education institutions, and broad educational policies do not take into account individual students' cultural contexts. The ecological model provides a framework for a comprehensive approach that reaches across student settings and offers a promising new perspective for understanding and promoting the development of college readiness strategies for all students and stakeholders.

Foreword

On this eve of the 2012 presidential election, with both major political parties offering solutions in their platforms for how to fix the problems that face American higher education, only one thing is clear: there is a problem that needs to be fixed. Indeed, when it comes to higher education, there are actually some points of agreement between the two major presidential parties: higher education is too expensive and the costs are rising too quickly; the pace and rate of graduation is too slow and too low; too many students are failing to meet their educational goals; and, for too long, higher education has not been held accountable for what students learn or if they are learning at all. The solutions offered, of course, differ. One party suggests that free market forces can fix what ails higher education, and the other suggests that some government intervention will provide solutions to the problem. We don't yet know who will win the election (although by the time this is published, we will know). We do know that the microscope is on higher education, and it must respond affirmatively.

Higher education (and those who work there) has been eager to play the blame game with regard to its woes. If only states supported higher education at the level that they once did (or should do). If only K–12 education adequately prepared students for the rigors of college. If only K–12 were more equitable and offered all of its graduates a sufficient and adequate level of educational preparation. If only college students worked harder and were more motivated to learn. If only.

If these conditions were met, higher education would have an easier job of graduating students, of making sure that they learned the right amount and the right content, and that a college education was worth the price it cost.

But the blame game isn't working, and the problems that affect higher education, the K–12 system, and the individual student aren't just going to go away. Higher education has to work with the cards it is dealt, and it has to deal with the academic preparation (or lack thereof) of its student body.

This monograph on college readiness by Karen Arnold, Elissa Lu, and Kelli Armstrong offers important information and perspectives to help higher education move beyond the blame game. It applies Urie Bronfenbrenner's sociological theory to the problem of college readiness and offers frameworks for understanding the multiple systems at play without letting higher education off the hook for trying to fix the problem. The theoretical framework is particularly useful because it helps to frame the problem of college readiness as systemic and multifaceted and suggests that simple quick fixes will not be sufficient. However, it doesn't leave us helplessly floundering in an unfixable system; rather, it helps to explain how the systems interlock and coordinate and provides some direction on what institutions of higher education can do.

Although this monograph focuses on explaining a theory and its use in research, it will be helpful to practitioners as well. Researchers, faculty members, graduate students, federal and state policymakers, and institutional leaders in both K–12 and higher education contexts will find this monograph to be of use. It is written for everyone interested in access to and success in higher education. There are a couple of other monographs in the series that overlap well with the topic and approach undertaken here. In particular, I recommend Amy Bergerson's (2009) monograph on college choice and access, Rachelle Winkle-Wagner's (2010) on cultural capital, Marybeth Walpole's (2007) on low socioeconomic students, and David Arendale's (2010) on remedial education. Each of these offers related but slightly different perspectives on this topic of college readiness.

No matter who wins the presidential race or what happens with regard to state and federal policy, higher education must figure this out. We have to better fulfill our promise of providing equitable and excellent postsecondary education. There is too much at stake to maintain the status quo.

Lisa E. Wolf-Wendel
Series Editor

Acknowledgments

We warmly thank the following individuals for their assistance in conceptualizing and carrying out this collaborative project:

Samantha Allen

Elizabeth Bracher

Paul Brown

Ben Castleman

Loretta Cedrone

Jill Claridge

Zachary Cole

Penny Hauser-Cram

Mario DeAnda

Kara Godwin

Jackie Lerner

Jennifer May

Ashley Moellinger

Esther Park

Kris Renn

Lynette Robinson

Pharlone Troussant

Marybeth Walpole

Katherine Lynk Wartman

Lisa Wolf-Wendel

Published online in Wiley Online Library
(wileyonlinelibrary.com) • DOI: 10.1002/aehe.20005

The Case for a Comprehensive Model of College Readiness

NEARLY ALL ENTERING NINTH GRADERS in the United States expect to attend college (Aud and others, 2010). When they leave high school, however, only 55 percent of students with diplomas enroll in a postsecondary institution. Although U.S. college enrollment rates are rising, gaps in college enrollment by family income are pronounced and remain stubbornly resistant to change (Bailey and Dynarski, 2011). And college enrollment is just the first step toward a postsecondary certificate or degree. The real goal is college success in the form of a postsecondary credential. Currently only 55.5 percent of students who enter four-year institutions graduate within six years, and only 29.2 percent of two-year college students graduate within three years (Knapp, Kelly-Reid, and Ginder, 2010). As with college enrollment numbers, U.S. rates of higher education persistence are a major problem, particularly for low-income students (Bowen, Chingos, and McPherson, 2009). There is widespread consensus that the leading cause of the low college entrance and success rates among "economically and educationally challenged students" (Walpole, 2007) is a lack of college readiness.

"College readiness" refers to a student's capacity to enroll at a postsecondary institution, take credit-bearing classes beginning in the first year, earn passing grades in courses, and persist to his or her educational goals. The American public, policymakers, educators, and employers are increasingly aware that a high school diploma does not signify that students are prepared to succeed in college. A large-sample analysis from ACT, for instance, concluded that only one in four high school graduates nationally is adequately prepared for college-level course work in core subjects (ACT, 2011).

Even meeting eligibility requirements and being accepted into a college or university does not mean students are college ready. Up to 60 percent of students at nonselective colleges and universities and 30 percent of students at somewhat selective colleges and universities meet their institutions' eligibility criteria but are not ready for college-level course work (Shulock, 2010). At highly selective institutions, one in ten entering students is academically unready for college. This gap between college-level expectations and entering students' skills results in one-third of students at four-year institutions and 42 percent of students at two-year institutions enrolling in remedial education course work (National Center for Education Statistics, 2012). Remedial course work is closely linked to reduced rates of retention and completion. Bridging students' transition to higher education by increasing their college readiness is therefore a major concern across American stakeholders, as well as globally (Thomas and Quinn, 2007).

Researchers, policymakers, and educational practitioners have addressed the movement from high school to college under many labels, including *college choice, college transition, college access, college success,* and *college preparation.* Whereas *college access* has traditionally referred to eligibility, acceptance, and enrollment in a postsecondary institution as distinct from not attending college (Perna, 2006), the emphasis on college preparation over the past decade has given way to the more general term *college readiness. College readiness* is an umbrella term that refers to the multidimensional set of skills, traits, habits, and knowledge that students need to enter college with the capacity to succeed once they are enrolled. College-ready students are adequately prepared with the psychosocial, academic, and practical skills and knowledge to "enroll and succeed—without remediation—in a credit-bearing course at a postsecondary institution that offers a baccalaureate program, or in a high-quality certificate program that enables students to enter a career pathway with potential future advancement" (Conley, 2010, p. 21). Success, according to Conley, means completion of the course; for certificate courses, success is demonstrated by proficiency or eligibility for subsequent required levels of work. Although academic preparedness is central to this concept and *academic preparation* and *college readiness* are often used interchangeably, they are not identical concepts (Barnes, Slate, and Rojas-LeBouef, 2010; Padilla,

2009b). The broader construct of *college readiness* includes the academic skills and practices that underlie academic performance, the practical knowledge to engage in college search activities, and the aspirations, motivation, and self-efficacy to attend college.

Voluminous research literature on college readiness has appeared over the past ten years, spread across foundation reports, government documents, practitioner publications, and scholarly sources in numerous disciplines. The research represents a wide array of definitions of key concepts, theoretical approaches, and methods (Perna, 2007; Perna and Thomas, 2008). Reports and empirical studies variously take students, demographic groups, programs, schools, states, and policies as their unit of analysis. Because of this diversity in investigators, publication outlets, and approaches, the literature on college readiness appears to exist in pockets of largely independent conversations under a number of labels.

College readiness programs are a major focus of research, policy, and practice concerning postsecondary access and success. Broadly, these programs attempt to reduce social inequality by providing the connections between K–12 and higher education that are necessary for economically and educationally challenged students to enter college and persist to a postsecondary degree. Begun over fifty years ago, readiness programs offered by government, schools, nonprofit, educational, and philanthropic organizations have proliferated over the past two decades (Swail, 2000). As in the broader literature on readiness, the knowledge base on school- and community-based readiness programs is incomplete and fragmented. Even the relatively rare instances of rigorous program evaluations have resulted in mixed findings about whether and how programs can help students access higher education. Like any other single factor within students' lives, college readiness programs alone have not been able to eliminate socioeconomic disparities in U.S. college access and success.

During the same period as this major research activity, the United States has seen intensive policy efforts, particularly at the state level, to increase the enrollment and degree attainment of students. The larger national educational reform and accountability movements have come to be centrally concerned with college readiness, which is now seen as identical to workplace readiness and essential for state and national well-being (Baker, Clay, and Gratama, 2005; Conley 2010; Obama, 2009; U.S. Department of Education, 2006). Policymakers and scholars have identified a set of persistent challenges that impede social mobility through higher education for the country's rising numbers of students who are from low-income households, underrepresented racial and ethnic groups, and families without previous experience in higher education (Bailey and Dynarski, 2011; Reardon, 2011). These challenges center on systematic group differences in students' academic preparation for postsecondary study, knowledge about negotiating pathways into and through higher education, and ability to secure the money to pay for college. To date, however, policy initiatives have made only modest inroads in eliminating national socioeconomic gaps in higher education or reducing the disproportionately high concentration of low-income students within less selective institutions and remedial courses (Arendale, 2010; Bowen, Chingos, and McPherson, 2009; Perna and Titus, 2004; St. John, 2007).

The Complexity of College Readiness

Despite widespread awareness of the problem, reams of topical research, substantial policy efforts, and thousands of college preparation programs, the achievement gap between affluent and low-income youth has actually widened since the late 1980s (Bailey and Dynarski, 2011). This discouraging state of affairs relates to the complexity of the problem and its embeddedness in larger social structures (Padilla, 2009b; Reardon, 2011).

Immigration patterns, U.S. income distribution, racism, and free-market ideology are just a few of the large forces in society that lie well beyond the reach of families and schools but frame students' actual and perceived opportunities and their college preparation behaviors (McDonough, 1997; Portes, 1999; Spencer, 2006). The structural arrangements of society that arise out of cultural beliefs and values are also outside the immediate lives of students but clearly affect them. For instance, government and higher education policies and priorities determine the affordability of higher education, while political considerations privilege the interests of middle-class and wealthy Americans over attention to poverty reduction. Residential segregation by race, ethnicity, and—particularly—family income affects the quality of schooling and other social structures that relate to educational achievement (Reardon, 2011). Time plays a role in this complex picture: students' educational experiences vary according to their age and generation, historical era, and time-bound events such as the economic recession or the rise of the educational accountability movement.

Closer at hand, even well-designed educational interventions are not pervasive: students participate in school and college preparation programs while simultaneously experiencing other roles, settings, and relationships. Students differ according to culture and other group characteristics. Within demographic groups, individuals vary in their personal qualities and experiences. In other words, individual students respond differently to the same environmental contexts. Importantly, individuals have at least some degree of influence in choosing and shaping their environments.

College readiness has to do with all of these simultaneously interacting forces of ideology, social and organizational structure, time, and individual agency. Considering this complex view, America's inability to solve the problem of social mobility through higher education is understandable. The pressing social problem of persistent socioeconomic and racial gaps in U.S. postsecondary attainment seems impossible to untangle without accounting for this complicated picture. What is needed, in short, is a way of making sense of the complexity of college readiness without simplifying it.

One way to move the field of college readiness forward, we suggest, is to use a framework that centers on the complexity of interacting environmental influences as the focal concern of college readiness programs, policies, and research—in other words, an ecological approach. This strategy requires a broad look at what is known about college readiness. To restrict a review to one aspect—for instance, college preparation programs—would be to replicate the problem of the field in which one element of college readiness is seen in isolation from the interconnected system to which it is tightly linked.

Mapping the research onto an ecological framework serves several purposes. First, this approach highlights the comprehensive nature of college readiness and provides a way to reconceptualize research, policy, and practice to account for the complexity of relationships between students and multiple environments. Second, the framework supplies a coherent organizational scheme for the large literature on college readiness. Third, an ecological analysis highlights gaps in what is known about particular environment levels and interactions across levels, enabling the development of a research agenda that has the potential to move the field in promising new directions. Fourth, the lens of ecology accounts for both structure and agency, providing a bridge across developmental, organizational, and policy approaches. Fifth, our work has the potential to inform improvement in practice through the potential of ecology theory to explain socioeconomic gaps in educational attainment and to guide school, college, and community-based preparation programs.

Quasi-Ecological Approaches to College Readiness

Leading researchers in the fields of college readiness and college success have begun that project by developing models that attempt to portray multiple environmental contexts in which individual, institutional, and societal factors exert influence on students' postsecondary choices and outcomes. Most notably, Laura Perna's influential model of college choice connects economic human capital views of cost and benefit calculations to sociological factors of internalized cultural attributes ("habitus") and social resources (Perna, 2006, 2007; Perna and Thomas, 2008). Perna's model includes four layers of the environmental context that operate on students' college choice decisions: (1) student habitus (later referred to as the "internal level" [Perna and Thomas, 2008]); (2) school and community context; (3) higher education context; and (4) social, economic, and policy context.

It is not clear to what extent the layers are theoretically nested within each other besides their ordering from closest to most distant from the experience of the precollege student. Mechanisms by which higher education and societal contexts affect students are not specified. The model does not focus on interactions and multidirectional influences among environments, for instance, in the ways that social forces form student habitus (Super and Harkness, 2002) or the ways in which students might influence their environments. In fact, the internal layer of the model mixes characteristics of the person with characteristics of his or her immediate environments, while the school level contains immediate and indirect environmental elements. Quantitative analyses of this model follow the common convention of controlling for covariation among components of college readiness to reveal main effects of individual factors in a directional model of inputs and outcomes. This analytical strategy minimizes an emphasis on multidirectional interactions among college readiness components. However, Perna's conception of college choice highlights the multiple contexts that influence student decisions, and the model could be revised to account for multidirectional effects among interacting environments.

Leading scholars, William Tierney and Kristan Venegas, have advanced a cultural ecology model that features four overlapping contexts: familial environments, educational environments, community environments, and out-of-class environments (Tierney and Venegas, 2007, 2009). Unlike the Perna model, the featured contexts are all environments in which the student has direct experience, and the framework highlights the ways in which the different contexts connect to each other. The focus of the Perna model on the individual and societal contexts is not included separately in the cultural ecology framework. In their discussion of familial contexts, Tierney and Venegas (2007) cite Bronfenbrenner's (1979) conceptualization of individual differences in agency that shape the ways in which students enter and experience their environments.

A final model that approaches an ecological perspective is Raymond Padilla's (2009a) expertise model of student success. This model identifies college success barriers (including college readiness barriers), formal academic and informal heuristic knowledge about how to succeed, and actions students take to put their knowledge into use to overcome barriers to success. Padilla's model corresponds closely to several ecological principles. For instance, the model acknowledges the embeddedness of student experience in layers of organizations, policy, and politics. In discussing theory, Padilla acknowledges the overarching role of ideology and culture, the importance of historical time, and individual student knowledge and motivational dispositions. The model stresses direct student experience in recognizing that "education occurs within the 'life world' . . . of everyday affairs, where people attend to the business of living" (2009a, p. 5). Padilla paraphrases ecological theory in his statement that "student success is an outcome of human interaction in complex educational systems, which in turn are embedded in complex social systems" (2009a, p. 1). He deliberately simplifies the complexity to drive practice, however, rather than exploiting the implications of his ecological insights.

The Next Generation of College Readiness Research

Developmental systems models in psychology offer well-established theories and associated research designs with the potential to move the field of college readiness forward. This family of theories describes the relations and processes linking the multiple, interacting elements within the total ecology of human development. The best-known and most influential of these theories is that of Urie Bronfenbrenner (1917-2005). Bronfenbrenner's ecological theory of human development is also known as the process-person-context-time (PPCT) model (1974, 1979, 1993, 2005; Bronfenbrenner and Morris, 2006; Moen, Elder, and Lüscher, 1995). The field of college readiness needs to account for all of the components in this model: the role of student individual characteristics and personal agency; the characteristics of multiple, interacting levels of context; the effects of chronological and historical time; and, above all, the processes through which all these elements effect change in students.

Though canonical in developmental psychology, Bronfenbrenner's model has been largely the province of child and family research. In higher education, the theory is beginning to appear in student affairs literature (Evans and others, 2010; Renn and Arnold, 2003). We introduce it here as a guide to the literature on college readiness in the hope that an established developmental systems approach will provide a comprehensive conceptual framework for the scattered field of college readiness.

Method and Organization

This monograph presents an analytical literature review of college readiness through the conceptual framework of Bronfenbrenner's ecological theory of human development. Although college readiness and college success are linked conceptually, we provide an overview of the wide literature on the person and environment factors, policies, and programs that relate to students' preparation and entrance into postsecondary education with the capacity for college success. We include dual-enrollment program designs in which high school students simultaneously enroll in high school and college courses. We do not address the college success literature, which we define as beginning with postsecondary matriculation by high school graduates or GED holders. For this reason, we omit the large literature on remedial education in colleges and universities.

The monograph focuses on the main populations and topics in the college readiness literature. The population of U.S. youth who are traditionally aged high school and college students dominates research; for the most part, we concentrate on literature about this population. Within this broad parameter, the review is centrally concerned with the economically and educationally challenged students identified by Walpole (2007) as "low-SES [socioeconomic status], low-income, working-class, and first-generation students" (p. 14). We extend this definition by including literature that focuses on underrepresented racial and ethnic groups within this larger population. We exclude research on high-SES college preparation activities, such as literature about the rise of college coaching or enrichment gap years, and do not cover non-U.S. students.

In deciding what to include, we followed the literature itself in accepting a variety of terms for college readiness. We reviewed over five hundred foundation and government reports, scholarly journal articles, books, and some professional and popular publications. Although we are confident that the resulting literature review includes the leading concepts and findings and represents the contours of the current field of college readiness, the large number of sources in the References is still far from a comprehensive inventory of the field. Instead, our purpose was to map the literature onto an ecological framework that would provide an analytical tool for a new understanding of college readiness that could guide the next generation of research, policy, and practice.

The remainder of the monograph is organized with this generative purpose in mind. Having made the case for a comprehensive, theoretically driven literature review and described our search and coding methods, we next present a full exposition of the ecological person-process-context-time model. The core of the monograph is an exposition of the literature that organizes the concepts and research findings of the field according to each nested environmental level in the theory. For each level, we explore the implications of the ecological approach for identifying gaps in research and increasing college readiness for economically and educationally challenged students. We conclude with a full ecological model of college readiness and an ecological agenda for the field.

The Human Ecology Framework

UNEQUAL ACCESS TO A COLLEGE DEGREE is a classic systems problem involving reciprocal interactions among individuals and their multiple, nested environments. Urie Bronfenbrenner's influential human ecology model meets the challenge of accounting for the complex picture of college access and success. Refined and extended over the past thirty years (Bronfenbrenner, 1974, 1979, 1986, 1993, 2001, 2005; Bronfenbrenner and Ceci, 1994; Bronfenbrenner and Morris, 2006; Moen, Elder, and Lüscher, 1995), the ecological process-person-context-time (PPCT) theory has generated an enormous volume of research and played a leading role in the paradigm shift to contextual, developmental systems models in psychology (Lerner, 2006). (Toward the end of his life, Bronfenbrenner changed the theory's title to "bioecological" to reflect the ways in which developmental processes encourage or inhibit an individual's inherited potential.) Figure 1 illustrates the major components of the ecological theory.

Principles of Development in Ecological Systems

Human ecology theory begins from the assumption that individuals and environments are inseparably intertwined. Development refers to change in individuals toward progressively more complex and adequate functioning in their environments. Student development, in this definition, consists of increasingly sophisticated and effective college readiness attributes, knowledge, and behaviors (Padilla, 2009b). Such changes occur through what

FIGURE 1
The Ecological Framework

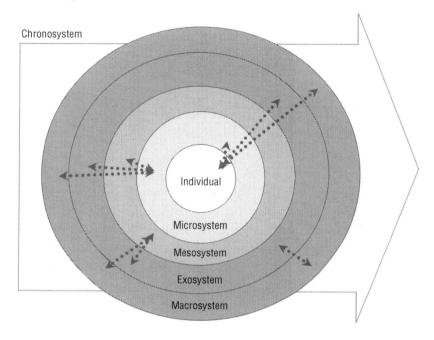

Bronfenbrenner calls "proximal processes," defined as "progressively more complex reciprocal interaction between an active, evolving, biopsychological human organism and the persons, objects, and symbols in its immediate environment" (Bronfenbrenner and Ceci, 1994, p. 572).

This dense definition warrants unpacking. First, individuals grow as a result of experiences in which they are challenged by encountering complexity. Responding attentively to another person is a source of complexity in an interpersonal encounter. Objects and symbols are challenging when they are "of a kind that invites attention, exploration, manipulations, elaboration, and imagination" (Bronfenbrenner and Morris, 2006, p. 798). Environments lacking challenge or those that are dysfunctional, chaotic, or overwhelming do not provide the experience of progressive complexity. Indeed, research demonstrates a strong relationship between negative personal outcomes and environmental disorder and dysfunction (Wachs, 1992). Overwhelming challenge is a likely cause of problems in college readiness for students who face multiple barriers to academic achievement and college access. As Bronfenbrenner notes, increasing complexity requires environmental encounters that occur at least somewhat regularly and are sustained.

Second, person-environment interactions are "reciprocal"; that is, a person produces his or her own development by acting on the context as well as being acted on by the environment. For example, a student's relative responsiveness to an interaction with a mentor will affect the behavior of the mentor toward the student. This is an especially important point in ecology theory—the "person" component of the PPCT equation. Individuals affect their contexts by the ways in which they selectively choose arenas of participation, seek out various degrees of challenge, and respond to the people and things with which they might interact. Even these individual differences in what Bronfenbrenner calls "developmentally instigative characteristics" are themselves formed as a result of environmental experiences, of course. For instance, African American students are vulnerable to stereotype threat (Steele and Aronson, 1995) because they have encountered expressions of the stereotype and are familiar with its predictions for their group's performance. As in this example, biological and demographic characteristics are important primarily through the ways in which they contribute to shaping a person's environmental interactions. The interactive nature of proximal processes suggests a strength-based perspective: environments do not determine student outcomes because they are constantly evolving through the agency of the person encountering them (Lerner, 2006).

Third, and finally, people develop only through experiences in their "immediate environment." Proximal processes are direct experiences with people (such as parents, teachers, and friends) or objects (like computers or books) or symbols (like language or art). More distant levels of the environment must be filtered through the individual's direct experience to constitute a proximal process. For instance, students experience the effects of school accountability legislation only in interactions within their immediate environment, such as test-oriented classroom instruction or the experience of taking a high-stakes examination.

Environmental Contexts

The next component of the model is context. Bronfenbrenner proposes that the direct interactions that make up proximal processes are a "joint function of the characteristics of the developing person [and] the environment—both immediate and more remote—in which the processes are taking place" (Bronfenbrenner and Morris, 2006, p. 798). The ecological model contains four nested levels of the environment ranging from the most immediate to the most distant: microsystem, mesosystem, exosystem, and macrosystem. The microsystem consists of the immediate social and physical environment, including the people, places, objects, symbols, and activities that an individual experiences directly. Padilla's (2009a) description of a "life world . . . of everyday affairs, where people attend to the business of living" (p. 5) is an excellent characterization of the microsystem. Family, school, and neighborhood are microsystems for students. Classrooms, peer groups, athletic teams, and college preparation programs are also student microsystems. So are social networking sites, coworkers at a job, school texts, neighborhood graffiti, and college information Web sites with which a student is directly in contact. An unread book, an unimplemented policy, and an unconsulted guidance counselor lie outside this layer: environmental elements that a student does not experience directly are not part of that student's microsystem. When they are not directly encountered, higher education lies outside high school students' microsystem. Changes in student college readiness, according to this view, can take place only in the "life world of everyday affairs" (Padilla, 2009a, p. 5). "All of the levels of environmental influence are filtered through microsystems, where actual experiences take place. *Proximal processes* . . . are essentially patterns of person-environment interactions in the *microsystem*" (Spencer, 2006, p. 866, italics in original).

Student development takes place through direct experience in immediate settings, but each individual experiences many settings, activities, and roles. Mesosystem interactions are connections across microsystems—the network of overlapping relationships, messages, objects, and symbols in a person's everyday world. The mesosystem is a crucial layer of the environment for college readiness because the totality of students' experiences determines their educational dispositions and behaviors. The relative importance of any particular microsystem varies within the mesosystem, as students dispense their time and emotional energy in various configurations of involvement. A student's investment of time working at a paid job, caring for siblings, or viewing social networking sites, for instance, means less time available for study (Perna, 2010). Or students might spend long hours in school but reserve their emotional intensity primarily for out-of-school relationships and activities. Equally germane to a mesosystem analysis is the way in which relationships and messages carry across different microsystems. Neighborhood friends might or might not appear in other settings as classmates and fellow college preparation program participants. Families vary in the degree to which they echo teachers' messages about academic achievement behaviors. Cultural knowledge might be reinforced or contradicted in school settings (Villalpando and Solorzano, 2005). One microsystem can change another, as when parenting practices predispose children to choose particular peer groups (Steinberg, Darling, and Fletcher, 1995) or teachers invite students into special programs. Theoretically, the most influential mesosystems are those that invite increasing complexity in microsystems and offer a high degree of overlap and congruence across the many facets of a student's life. This proposition suggests that the lack of success in college readiness might result from inconsistent and contradictory membership and messages in a student's everyday arenas.

The exosystem describes the level of the environment in which individuals are not physically present but where events occur that indirectly affect processes in their immediate settings (Bronfenbrenner, 1993). For example, students are rarely in direct contact with their family members' workplaces, but their immediate experience is affected by the schedule, pay, distance, and work conditions of their parents' jobs. The parenting practices in the families of students' friends offer an example of another exosystem factor that has been found to affect adolescents' academic achievement (Steinberg, Darling, and Fletcher, 1995). The worlds of higher education institutions and related policy organizations and decision makers are similarly distant from a student's personal experience yet instrumental in shaping it. Much of the research and policy work in higher education describes environments that lie in the exosystem of students: policies, institutional and organizational systems, laws and regulations, and educational program models and designs. The exosystem also encompasses social structures such as community characteristics, the relationship between educational credentials and the labor force, and the organization of social services and postsecondary financial aid. Curriculum alignment policies and partnerships between high schools and colleges are examples of key college readiness efforts that take place in the student's exosystem. Close attention to this level of the environment is warranted because it is here that politicians, policymakers, and educators can design structural and program interventions for the purpose of decreasing socioeconomic gaps in college readiness. However, it bears repeating that change can occur only when exosystem factors make their way into the student microsystem, where they will have differential effects according to the way in which an individual engages a particular immediate environment and how that setting interacts with other parts of his or her life.

The broadest level of the ecological environment is the macrosystem, comprising ideology, culture, and major social institutions such as government, religion, and the economy. The shape of social stratification in the United States, for instance, is a macrosystem factor, as are ideologies of individualism, capitalism, and meritocracy. Globalism is another macrolevel element of human ecology. The ideology of accountability and the belief that higher education is a private good are additional examples of macrolevel social values animating educational institutions. As Tierney and Venegas (2009) have pointed out, theory itself is a form of ideology that shapes assumptions and practices in college access. In addition, the macrosystem contains language, metaphors, and large concepts that construct experience. Racism, sexism, and anti-immigrant ideologies emerge from the macrosystem and are tightly coupled with language systems of difference and deficit (Iverson, 2012). Members of ethnic minority groups experience both the macrosystem of the dominant culture and that of their particular subculture.

All of the other levels of the ecology exist within the macrosystem. Macrosystems can and do change, however, as a result of pressures within other levels of the environment. Most clearly, they change as a function of time—the final component of the PPCT model. The chronosystem affects all levels of the environment and the ways in which individuals interact with their ecosystem. The metaphor of "pathway" or "pipeline" dominates the college readiness conversation, suggesting that college access and success is a longitudinal process requiring steps that must be achieved at particular times and in a particular order (Cabrera and La Nasa, 2001; Lumina Foundation, 2009; Tierney and Venegas, 2007).

In addition to addressing the importance of timing in life transitions, the chronosystem identifies the effects of changing social contexts within historical time. Student lives occur within historical eras and in age cohorts that experience historical events in particular ways (Elder and Shanahan, 2006). For instance, low-income students who graduated from U.S. high schools in 2008 experienced a period of high college tuition at a moment in which it was particularly difficult to obtain private loans because of tightened credit in the aftermath of a financial crisis. The aspect of linked lives (Elder and Shanahan, 2006) in financing higher education appeared for many students in the convergence of their need for college funding with recession-related financial strain on their family. In response to the constraints of that particular historical moment, many low-income students postponed the transition from high school to college, but this action meant a sociologically off-time life transition that decreased their chances of attaining a degree.

Environmental Interactions: A Fully Ecological Model

The ecological model of human development can clarify and extend understanding of college readiness through its careful delineation of levels of the environment and provide a model of the mechanisms and role of human agency in processes of change in students' immediate environment. The full complexity of a human ecosystem, however, lies in the multidirectional connections across environments, and it is here that Bronfenbrenner's theory has its full expression. "The levels are conceptualized as *more* than just interacting; instead they are seen as integrally fused together. Behavior and its development are melded as ever-changing sets of *relationships* and the history of these relationships over time. Thus, causality is multiply determined over levels and continually changing over time" (Thelen and Smith, 2006, p. 267, italics in original).

Instead of the current practice of isolating important factors of college readiness as targets for policy and intervention (Wachs, 1992), the developmental systems approach features methodology that investigates the connections among these factors: *"In ecological research, the principal main effects are likely to be interactions"* (Bronfenbrenner, 1979, p. 38, italics in original). A focus on environmental interactions highlights questions such as how students experience policies or program designs in their lives, how the settings in an individual's life connect, and how individuals optimize their own development in choosing and responding to environments.

Individual: The Attributes of College Readiness

ACCORDING TO ECOLOGICAL THEORY, individuals develop their college readiness through reciprocal interactions with their environments. Biological, cognitive, emotional, and behavioral characteristics shape individuals' interactions with their surrounding environments and can indirectly instigate the development of college readiness. Although they do not determine a student's future, developmentally instigative characteristics serve as "sources of variation in the person's susceptibility to the developmental effects of environmental conditions and of enduring patterns of interaction in the person and his or her immediate environment (i.e., proximal processes)" (Bronfenbrenner, 1995, p. 633). In other words, individuals vary in their characteristic ways of selecting, experiencing, and instigating responses from their environments. It is these differences, rather than static group-level demographic traits, "that are most powerful in affecting the course and outcome of subsequent development" (Bronfenbrenner, 2005, p. 94). Developmentally instigative characteristics influence individuals' subsequent experiences and are partly formed by experience. In this sense, individuals are simultaneously products and producers of their environments. High academic aspirations, for example, may result from family and school experiences while also driving student decisions and behaviors that affect subsequent experiences.

This chapter focuses on the developmentally instigative characteristics that constitute college readiness—study skills, self-efficacy, aspirations, and academic preparedness—and explores how they synergistically influence individuals' readiness (Cabrera and La Nasa, 2000; Perna, 2005; Rueda, 2005).

FIGURE 2
Key Elements of College Readiness

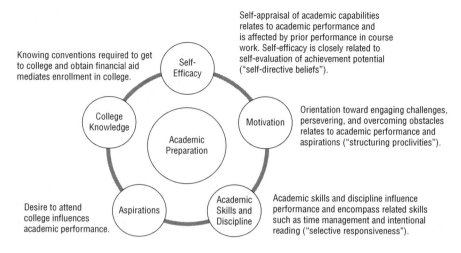

Self-appraisal of academic capabilities relates to academic performance and is affected by prior performance in course work. Self-efficacy is closely related to self-evaluation of achievement potential ("self-directive beliefs").

Knowing conventions required to get to college and obtain financial aid mediates enrollment in college.

Orientation toward engaging challenges, persevering, and overcoming obstacles relates to academic performance and aspirations ("structuring proclivities").

Desire to attend college influences academic performance.

Academic skills and discipline influence performance and encompass related skills such as time management and intentional reading ("selective responsiveness").

Self-Efficacy

College Knowledge

Academic Preparation

Motivation

Aspirations

Academic Skills and Discipline

Academic preparation includes proficiency in (Conley, 2010):

• Subject matter knowledge: English language arts, writing, math, sciences, and social sciences
• Cognitive skills: problem formulation, research, interpretation, communication of well-reasoned arguments, precision, and accuracy
• General academic skills: reading and writing a variety of texts and styles

Sources: Conley (2010); Mattern and Shaw (2010); Perna (2005); Robbins and others (2004, 2006); Rueda (2005).

While relatively few students leave high school well developed in every component of college readiness, individuals' strengths in a particular area can bolster college access and success (see Figure 2).

Developmentally instigative characteristics influence development in three key ways. First, *resource characteristics* are abilities, knowledge, and skills that enable individuals to engage in developmentally more complex interactions with their environments (Bronfenbrenner and Morris, 2006). For instance, students' knowledge about financial aid contributes to a view that college is a possibility and compels them to prepare for college. Similarly, students' foundational content knowledge of subject matter enables them to learn more advanced concepts within the discipline.

Second, *force characteristics* predispose the ways individuals choose to respond to their environment. These characteristics manifest as "differential interests, values, belief systems, and goals in relation to persons, objects, and symbols in the environment and in relation to the self" (Bronfenbrenner, 1995, p. 634). Among force characteristics, structuring proclivities lead individuals to seek out varying degrees of complexity in their environments. Directive beliefs or perceptions about their own agency are additional force characteristics that inform individuals' behaviors and expectations about the likely result of their actions. For example, individuals who have a strong sense of academic self-efficacy might be more inclined to take advanced course work. Individuals who plan to go to college might attend their school's college fairs, engage in more cocurricular activities, and seek out information about the college admissions process.

Finally, individuals' *demand characteristics* encompass the attributes affecting the responses individuals invite or elicit from their environments. For example, students who exhibit high academic motivation or college aspirations might receive greater attention from their teachers in the classroom as well as recommendations for special college preparatory experiences.

A review of the literature demonstrates the ways in which academic preparedness, college knowledge, study skills, self-efficacy, and aspirations serve as resource, force, and demand characteristics influencing the development of college readiness.

Resource Characteristics

College readiness is a developmental process that leverages prior learning, experiences, and skills. Individuals' experiences, biological characteristics, and abilities serve as resources that predispose individuals to a particular developmental trajectory relative to their developmental stage. In developing college readiness, an understanding of college costs and the application process, along with academic preparedness, orients students toward considering college as a possibility and enables them to perform at the required academic levels.

Academic Preparation

To be considered college ready, students are expected to master core concepts in key subject areas and acquire ways of thinking. The process of learning is dynamic and additive, with prior knowledge influencing students' subsequent ability to acquire more advanced academic concepts as well as the likelihood that they will do so (Resnick, 1983). The cognitive effort required to acquire new and related content decreases when knowledge is already stored and organized in schemata. For this reason, prior learning experiences, familiarity with problems, chunking, and other cognitive processes enable individuals to acquire information more easily and learn more effectively (van Merrienboer and Ayres, 2005). Learning advanced topics and concepts requires increasingly more complex structures of thinking, notably abstract thinking, that arise through stages of intellectual development (Piaget, 1970). Conley (2010) names the key cognitive strategies that underlie ways of knowing that are required for success in college-level course work, including problem formulation, research, interpretation, communication of well-reasoned arguments, precision, and accuracy. Similarly, the National Research Council (2002) identifies the expectation that college students be able to draw inferences, interpret results, examine various explanations, solve complex problems, draw conclusions, collaborate in group work, conduct and present research, and think deeply. Conley (2010) also emphasizes the importance of broad, interdisciplinary academic skills such as reading and distinguishing among various textual formats, writing in multiple rhetorical modes, editing, and rewriting. Individual development on these dimensions comes about through practice and results in the ability to succeed in tasks of progressively greater complexity. Such skills also assist individuals in learning more advanced concepts in key subject areas. The concepts within the major disciplines of English, mathematics, sciences, and social sciences present students with a sequence of increasing complexity of required skills and knowledge. Through acquiring a foundational understanding of algebraic expressions and geometry, for example, individuals are positioned to succeed in trigonometry and college calculus. Organizational structures such as grade levels also reinforce the sequential nature of knowledge in the disciplines.

Academic Habits

Academic habits, such as self-management, self-awareness, self-monitoring, and self-discipline, constitute another set of actions and skills students need to master academic content and concepts. These traits underlie study skills such as the ability to record, organize, synthesize, remember, and use information (Hoover and Patton, 1995). In turn, study skills strongly influence college academic performance. The ability to estimate the time it takes to complete assignments and the ability to study effectively are also important to success as a student (Lammers, Onwuegbuzie, and Slate, 2001). Presumably a student with stronger academic habits is better able to allocate time, energy, and resources to mastering content. Subsequently, such a student is more likely to become academically prepared, learn the college admissions process, and develop college readiness.

In an examination of ACT test takers' data, Robbins and others (2006) defined academic self-discipline as the amount of time students spend on course work and how much they see themselves exerting effort to complete homework. Researchers found that academic self-discipline correlates positively with high school grade point average and ACT composite scores. Student self-discipline was a much better predictor of achievement than demographic categories in the areas of college academic performance and postsecondary retention. Self-discipline is tied closely to motivation; both concern students' selective responsiveness to academic tasks. Students are most successful when they demonstrate engagement, self-regulation, and self-determination in choosing to complete assignments when they are willing to expend their best effort (Robbins and others, 2006).

Despite the importance of developing strong academic study skills, study skills are not necessarily taught in schools (Zimmerman, 1998). Academic study behaviors and associated personal traits all require practice and training, as studying is an intentional activity that typically occurs outside formal learning environments (Gettinger and Seibert, 2002). Environmental interactions and personal qualities are mutually constituting: the development of academic behaviors can be self-reinforcing, as in the case of students whose positive results from academic behaviors increase their motivation to develop more advanced skills.

College Knowledge

"College knowledge" (Conley, 2005) influences individuals' academic behaviors, including their likelihood of eventual enrollment in college (Berkner and Chavez, 1997; Cabrera and La Nasa, 2000; Hossler, Schmit, and Vesper, 1999). Understanding what college is, how to choose colleges, and how to pay for higher education are enormously complex concepts. Developing the knowledge to navigate the complicated pathway to college is especially challenging for students without a family history of higher education. Like academic knowledge, knowledge about higher education involves a hierarchy of information, skills, and required supports. The development of college knowledge is particularly important because the traditional college admissions process is time sensitive, and preparation begins as early as eighth grade, when students make decisions about enrollment in college preparatory course work (Cabrera and La Nasa, 2000).

A significant body of literature has examined student and family comprehension of college costs, financial aid availability, and aid application procedures (Long, 2007; McDonough and Calderone, 2006; Roderick, Nagaoka, Coca, and Moeller, 2008; Tierney and Venegas, 2009). Variability in individual levels of college knowledge can result in differential college trajectories. In one study of Chicago Public School seniors, Roderick, Nagaoka, Coca, and Moeller (2008) found that filling out a Free Application for Federal Student Aid was an early predictor of enrolling in a four-year college. Similarly, an analysis of National Education Longitudinal Study (NELS) data found that a higher proportion of economically and educationally disadvantaged black and Latino students who had received information about financial aid from one or two sources were more likely than other college-qualified individuals to take active steps to enroll in college (Berkner and Chavez, 1997).

College knowledge varies by socioeconomic status and parental experience with higher education. In a study of Boston and local area high school students, Avery and Kane (2004) found that only half of Boston Public School seniors had obtained an application to their first-choice college by the fall of their last year of high school, compared to 91 percent of fellow students at wealthier suburban schools. The actions of the suburban students reflect their greater cultural and social capital as the children of college-educated parents who are deeply familiar with the college selection and admission process (Winkle-Wagner, 2010). In contrast, would-be first-generation students and their families are unfamiliar with how a college campus works or how to finance their education (Arnold and others, 2009; Thayer, 2000). At the aggregate level, Latino and black students have less college knowledge than white and Asian students (Tornatzky, Cutler, and Lee, 2002).

Force Characteristics

Force characteristics set in motion the ways that individuals engage with their environments and therefore the ways that they experience proximal processes of development. Individuals exert agency over the development of their college readiness when they choose to take an advanced math class to earn college credits in high school or, conversely, opt for the easiest math class because it requires less effort. Individuals' perceptions of their abilities and the probability of earning a college degree can also influence their behaviors in ways that support the development of college readiness. Bronfenbrenner cites Bandura's self-efficacy theory as an example of individuals' likelihood to seek out more challenging environments as a result of beliefs in their abilities (Bronfenbrenner, 2005). Similarly, research suggests that college aspirations serve as another developmentally instigative characteristic that shapes interactions with the environment.

Self-Efficacy

Self-efficacy refers to the belief that one is capable of acting in ways that will achieve desired ends (Bandura, 1997). This belief affects students' understanding and feelings about their abilities and therefore mediates their decisions and actions about whether and how to prepare for college (Bandura, 1997). Self-efficacy is shaped by the messages individuals receive and their experiences over time. As students feel more capable, they are more likely to engage in tasks of greater complexity, such as rigorous course work. They are also more likely to see themselves as capable of going to college and more likely to follow through with their plans for higher education.

Positive self-efficacy has been found to account for nearly one-quarter of the variance in academic achievement (Pajares, 2006) and is also positively correlated to adjustment in college (Brady-Amoon and Fuertes, 2011). A meta-analysis of college outcome predictors found strong relationships between academic self-efficacy and cumulative college grade point average, even after controlling for socioeconomic status, high school grades, and standardized test scores (Robbins and others, 2004). Similarly, an examination of College Board data found a strong relationship between high school students' perceptions of their own efficacy and their academic performance in the first year of college (Mattern and Shaw, 2010).

Like all other developmentally instigative characteristics, self-efficacy is both the product of interactions with the environment and the producer of environment effects; positive self-efficacy is shaped by the outcomes of prior course work and influences subsequent academic performance. Among engineering students, for example, prior course work and engineering-related hobbies influence self-efficacy (Fantz, Siller, and DeMiranda, 2011). In another study, Dweck (2000) found that college undergraduates' views of their intelligence can be positively influenced if academic learning highlights their strengths. Dweck also found that students who believe that intelligence is changeable instead of fixed are more likely to improve their skills and take advantage of learning opportunities. Individual-level beliefs are formed through personal experience but also through social views of groups. For instance, gendered beliefs about math competence persist, with males overestimating their math abilities compared to females with the same grades and test scores (Correll, 2001).

Self-appraisal, or self-rated ability, is another area related to self-efficacy (Brady-Amoon and Fuertes, 2011). Understanding one's strengths and limitations helps students choose appropriate activities and settings and enables them to seek out and benefit from support when they need it (Mattern and Shaw, 2010; Sedlacek, 2004). Individuals also make different appraisals of the opportunities and hazards in their environments. Human capital and rational choice economic theories conceptualize students' analysis of costs and benefits in college, including the perceived likelihood of succeeding in college, as influencing their enrollment decisions (St. John, Cabrera, Nora, and Asker, 2001).

Aspirations

Aspiring to go to college is a central motivating factor driving college readiness. Presumably the more an individual desires a college degree, the more likely he or she is to engage in preparatory behaviors such as finding out information about admissions requirements, doing homework, and participating in college readiness programs. The research literature supports the association between aspirations and other components of college readiness. Mattern and Shaw (2010) found a relationship between SAT takers' degree aspirations and their college examination scores and academic achievement in high school and the first year of college. Generally students' educational attainment expectations correspond with their academic performance. Other researchers recognize that aspirations or plans alone do not guarantee academic preparation but do relate to college enrollment outcomes (Adelman, 1999; St. John, 1991). Evaluations of college preparation programs have confirmed relationships between anticipating college enrollment and academic preparedness (Gandara, 2002; Lozano, Watt, and Huerta, 2009).

Aspirations are socially constructed. Some studies have found that aspirations differ across students in different demographic subgroups. For example, some research has found that first-generation students have lower aspirations than other groups of students (Pascarella, Pierson, Wolniak, and Terenzini, 2004). Economically and educationally challenged students are less likely than wealthier groups to report that they expect to attend college (Berzin, 2010; McCarthy and Kuh, 2006). Other literature has explored gender differences in aspirations and found that higher career aspirations among females emerge as early as elementary and middle school. Blackhurst and Augur (2008) found that girls are more likely than boys to aspire to careers that require a college degree. Given the motivating influence of career goals on academic achievement and skills development, Blackhurst and Augur (2008) underline in their recommendations the importance of students' development of an early awareness of their abilities, interests, and abilities.

Demand Characteristics

In addition to influencing environmental interactions, individuals' developmentally instigative characteristics elicit responses from the surrounding environments. For example, teachers might refer individuals who exhibit high levels of academic discipline or college aspirations to college preparation programs or extracurricular opportunities. Similarly, students who demonstrate greater understanding of academic subject matters might be placed in higher-level classes. Bronfenbrenner (2005) discusses the role of appearance in influencing adults' treatment of youth. Research also suggests that student race can influence educators' instructional practices.

Much of the literature examining how student characteristics elicit differential responses from teachers is concentrated in elementary and middle schools. In one study, Skinner and Belmont (1993) found that elementary school students who exhibited high engagement in the classroom at the beginning of the school year later received greater support and involvement from instructors than more passive students. In contrast, less initially engaged students experienced more neglect, coercion, and inconsistent instruction from teachers. In another study, Tournaki (2003) reported that elementary and middle school teachers used social information such as students' level of attention in class to predict students' academic performance, but also used performance on reading exams to predict students' social behaviors. Based on their preconceived notions about students' abilities, these studies suggest that teachers might treat low- and high-ability students differently and reinforce cycles of behavior, such that students who are initially more inclined to engage in the classroom are further encouraged to engage in the classroom and less engaged students are further discouraged from participating in class.

Other research has illustrated how demographic characteristics influence teachers' treatment of students. Based on classroom observations, Irvine (1986) discovered that teachers' treatment of students varied by students' race and gender. Males received less feedback from teachers than females did. Differences also varied by race, with black females having fewer opportunities to respond to questions in the class than black males. In his review of NELS 1988 panel data, Dee (2005) took teacher characteristics into account and found that teachers are more likely to view students from racial backgrounds different from their own and the opposite sex as inattentive in class and less likely to complete homework, compared to students who matched teachers' race and sex.

The Individual in an Ecological Context

Both the environment and developmentally instigative characteristics serve as powerful forces shaping individuals' interactions with the environment and the course of human development. Each level of the ecology affects the individual's developmentally instigative attributes. For example, the macrosystem shapes the belief systems that individuals hold in the context of the surrounding culture, social structures, and systems (Bronfenbrenner, 2005). Poor academic behaviors can signal individual-level, interactional, or environmental issues, such as weak motivation, low engagement, or problematic family support (Gettinger and Seibert, 2002). As Bronfenbrenner (1993) notes, developmentally instigative characteristics "may be thought of as 'putting a spin' on a body in motion. The effect of that spin depends on the other forces, and resources, in the total ecological system" (p. 14).

When environments are rich with resources and structures that promote college readiness, students are more likely to develop the requisite skills and knowledge they need to succeed in college. In contrast, negative school experiences can serve as obstacles to the progressive acquisition of college-level content knowledge and contribute to a student's decision to drop out of high school (Eckstein and Wolpin, 1999). We next delve into features of the microsystem that can develop students' attributes of college readiness.

Microsystem: The Direct Experience of Students

IN THE ECOLOGICAL MODEL, there is only one way in which college readiness is directly shaped: through the individual's interactions within his or her immediate settings, or microsystems. According to Bronfenbrenner (1993), the microsystem is the "pattern of activities, roles, and interpersonal relations experienced by the developing persons" (p. 15). Microsystem settings contain features that "invite, permit, or inhibit engagement in sustained, progressively more complex interaction with, and activity in, the immediate environment" (Bronfenbrenner, 1993, p. 15). A rich microsystem has the potential to develop different dimensions of students' college readiness and engage them in tasks of greater complexity. The experiences of students in their immediate settings can deepen or diminish their academic preparation, academic habits, motivation, self-efficacy, aspirations, and college knowledge or cause these to stagnate.

The college preparation literature has centered on the people, settings, and programs situated around the student: peers, family, teachers, counselors, schools, and preparation programs. These settings serve as microsystems that can provide varying opportunities to develop college readiness (Kimura-Walsh, Yamamura, Griffin, and Allen, 2009; Padilla, 2009b; Perna, 2006). In addition to interactions with people, direct connections with social media and extracurricular activities are microsystems that can influence the development of motivation, self-efficacy, college knowledge, and academic preparation. Importantly, the influence of particular individuals and relationships varies across students and critical periods. For example, school counselors might play a minimal role in young high school students' lives in comparison to peers, but as students consider going to college, counselors' influence might increase with time (Bell, Rowan-Kenyon, and Perna, 2009). Because development occurs through proximal processes in students' microsystems, the literature offers practices to maximize student engagement in school classrooms, preparation programs, and cocurricular activities and discusses the impact of relationships with teachers, counselors, families, and peers in support of developing college readiness.

Academic Preparation in Schools

With academic preparation at the heart of college readiness, middle schools and high schools play a pivotal role in students' cognitive and content development. Classroom environments that support students' academic growth have been summarized as possessing the three Rs: rigor, relevance, and relationships (Levine, 2002; Mitchell and others, 2005). The body of literature on effective school and classroom design indicates that students benefit from access to classes with advanced academic content and classroom practices that are aligned with college classrooms' practices (Adelman, 2006; Conley, 2010). Schools that promote college readiness also offer academic and social supports to their students, such as learning communities and teachers and counselors who offer strong guidance through the college choice process. Table 1 summarizes findings about best school and classroom practices for college readiness.

Course Work

As Table 1 implies, more extensive exposure to major subject areas and progressively more advanced course work correspond to higher levels of academic preparedness. Conley (2005) and associations such as the Partnership for Assessment of Readiness for Colleges and Careers have mapped the content students need to master in order to be college ready. Taking four years of English, three years of math, two and a half years of sciences, and two years each of social sciences and foreign languages exposes students to the advanced academic concepts associated with eventual college completion (Adelman, 2006). This connection between high school course taking and college success is particularly pronounced for blacks and Latinos (Adelman, 2006;

TABLE 1
Strategies to develop college readiness in school contexts

Practice	Description
Teach Rigorous Content Aligned with College Expectations	Align curriculum with college-level coursework and provide assignments that grow in complexity. Instruction should strongly promote oral and written communication and require students to think scientifically, historically, and mathematically.
	Require students to take courses that are needed for general education, introductory-level college courses.
	Provide students with access to college-level coursework, such as Advanced Placement courses or dual-enrollment options.
	Expose students to subject matter content throughout the school year and for extended lengths of time in the school day with double blocked schedules.
	Offer freshman seminars and special remedial classes for incoming students who are already lagging behind in key subject areas like math or English.
	Assess students' prior knowledge and conceptions in subject areas along with their college knowledge.
	Integrate college assessments within high school exams.
Create Engaging Learning Environments	Personalize the learning experience for students, and consider using creative forms of instruction such as project-based learning.
	Draw on a set of instructional techniques designed to accelerate learning, such as classroom talk, collaborative and literacy work groups, and journaling.
	Provide connections to the workplace, and help students develop high career aspirations.
	Embed opportunities for empowering students through community-based projects.
Instruct Students in Academic Skill Areas	Teach and expect students to use study skills, academic discipline, and other academic behaviors.
	Increase student responsibility over their learning over time.

(Continued)

TABLE 1 (continued)

Practice	Description
Build a School-wide College-going Culture	Require students to take the SAT or ACT, and schedule it during a time when there is minimal chance of scheduling conflicts for working students.
	Generate and maintain a college-going culture where every staff member takes responsibility for getting students to college.
	Integrate college knowledge and college application activities into course work and other in-school activities.
	Ensure advisers have access to students' standardized test scores to tailor advising.
	Offer preparation counseling and activities in one-on-one and group settings.
	Help ensure that students understand college admissions requirements before entering high school.
Provide Holistic, Social Support	Help students build a network of supports across a number of individuals and mentors, including a network of caring adults who can mentor students.
	Provide culturally relevant environments and activities.
	Offer comprehensive and intensive long-term supports that take into account students' personal barriers and the time it takes to develop students' trust.
	Provide small learning communities or faculty advisories to enhance students' perceptions that their teachers know and care about them.

Sources: Adelman (2006); American Youth Policy Forum (1997); Conley (2010); Dounay (2008); Farmer-Hinton (2010); Garvey and Grobe (2011); Herlihy (2007); Le and Frankfort (2011); Martinez and Klopott (2005); McClafferty and McDonough (2000); Militello and others (2009); Nodine (2009); Quint, Thompson, and Bald (2008); Zelkowski (2010).

McCormick and Lucas, 2011). In other studies, enrollment in math classes following Algebra 2 is an important predictor of college performance (Berry, 2003). Long, Iatarola, and Conger (2009) found that the number of math courses taken corresponds with 75 percent of the readiness gap between Asian and white students. Furthermore, enrolling in Advanced Placement courses or International Baccalaureate classes provides direct alignment with college-level course work. Taking more than one Advanced Placement class is also associated with future completion of a bachelor's degree (Adelman, 2006).

Notably, it is not only the total number of years students take course work in major subject areas in high school, but also the consistent exposure to academic content throughout the course of an academic year that enhances individuals' subject matter knowledge. A review of 1988 National Education Longitudinal Study and 2005 National Assessment of Educational Progress High School Transcript Study data indicates that students taking fifty-minute classes every day over an entire academic year scored two-thirds of a grade level higher than students who took four ninety-minute classes every day for only one semester (Zelkowski, 2010). These findings correspond with the ecological theory proposition that development occurs as a result of proximal processes in which an individual encounters sustained experiences of increasing complexity.

Despite the importance of progressive complexity, access to higher-level academic content is not equitable across socioeconomic groups (Reardon, 2011). Adelman (2006) found that Latino and low-income students were adversely affected by the disparity in advanced mathematics course offerings across schools: approximately 72 percent of high schools in the wealthiest communities offered calculus courses compared to 44 percent of high schools in communities with higher poverty levels. School conditions mediate students' access to learning in multiple ways. A school's lack of resources manifests in microsystems with a dearth of school materials, crowded classrooms, and limited advanced course work. Such settings are perceived by students as dampening their learning opportunities (Kimura-Walsh, Yamamura, Griffin, and Allen, 2009).

Pedagogy

Within the classroom, carefully constructed learning environments form microsystems that can help bridge the gap between the content and cognitive strategies required in high school and college courses (Conley, 2010). Challenging assignments and purposeful pedagogy deepen students' skills and knowledge in the dimensions of college readiness, boost college performance, and compensate for gaps in academic knowledge (Tornatzky, Cutler, and Lee,

2002; Warburton, Bugarin, Nuñez, and Carroll, 2001). Because many instructional strategies are challenging to quantify, researchers frequently draw on case studies of alternative school environments.

In six college-oriented middle and high school learning environments that Conley (2010) profiled, students completed tasks that grow in complexity over the course of four years until they mirror college-level skills. For example, students at University Park Campus School in Worcester, Massachusetts, are asked to develop higher-order thinking and multiple writing styles beginning in the seventh grade. To demonstrate their critical thinking skills, for instance, middle schoolers complete an assignment in which they perform a literary analysis of picture books. In ninth grade, students are placed in small, semester-long courses with a strong focus on core subjects and few electives to build their foundational content knowledge. In their junior- and senior-year seminars, students write their college admission essays, complete college and financial aid applications, and go through the admissions process together. Similarly, the curriculum for entering ninth graders in Talent Development high schools—a model of reformed schools that aims to increase achievement in non-selective, comprehensive high schools—is carefully designed to move students into more advanced course work. Freshmen spend longer periods of time in key subject areas than other courses to build their foundational content knowledge. In addition, first-year students take a seminar class where they develop study skills, set goals, and build social skills they need for high school (Herlihy, 2007). Students who are underperforming by two or more grade levels take Transition to Math and Strategic Reading classes to strengthen their comprehension of key knowledge and skills they need to succeed in second-semester algebra and English.

Certain instructional styles appear to be particularly effective in helping students to deepen their academic knowledge and skills. In their observations of early colleges, Le and Frankfort (2011) identified collaborative group work, literacy groups, questioning, classroom talk, writing to learn, scaffolding, and structured supports in the classroom day as instructional strategies that propel students forward on a college path. Through collaborative and literacy group work, for example, students complete specific assigned tasks in which they collaborate to support classmates' learning and take responsibility for their own contributions in analyzing complex texts (Le and Frankfort, 2011). When teachers use questioning and classroom discussion, students state their beliefs or assumptions, critically think through problems aloud, and take risks in solving problems such as contradictory experimental results. Regular writing about what they learn or providing written guidance to absent or confused classmates enables students to clarify their own understanding and develop metacognitive skills. Overall, instruction is most effective when it fosters an environment of intellectual curiosity and increased student responsibility for their own learning.

In other examples, college readiness is embodied through project-based learning (Conley, 2010). Proximal processes requiring initiative, analysis, interpretation, and time management are characteristic of project-based learning. At Minnesota New Country School, students undertake multiple projects that they self-design and plan with an adviser (Conley, 2010). For their senior year, student projects require three hundred hours of project time and include a community presentation. In college preparation seminars, students read more texts than a typical high school class does and work on fewer assignments that increase in intensity throughout the term (Conley, 2010).

College-Going Culture

Many schools and classrooms that promote college readiness also involve students in a strong college-going culture that spans activities and brings college directly into students' experience. In some schools, students "adopt" a college that they investigate through class projects, campus visits, and required career pathways courses (Farmer-Hinton, 2010; Nodine, 2010). In examining the Creating a College Culture project, McClafferty and McDonough (2000) describe how students can take the PSAT examination on Tuesdays instead of Saturdays, so that the exam will not conflict with work schedules. Students' access to college resources in schools also facilitates their awareness of the college choice process. Positive college enrollment effects have been found in particular for black and Latino students from schools that offer a clearinghouse of college information to all students rather than only top academic performers (Hill, 2008).

Career Focus

Career awareness has been the focus of efforts connecting school to the real world. According to career development theory (Super, 1990), high school students are at the cusp of exploring potential careers and developing self-concepts based in part on imagined adult vocational roles. Self-discovery and exploration of career interests can help students become motivated to develop their college readiness if a college degree is required for their desired profession. Students at Big Picture Learning high schools, for instance, are motivated by workplace internships connected to the curriculum and provide real-world relevance and career exploration (Levine, 2002). Students in this national network of schools spend time each week in an internship in a field that they see as a potential career and complete a project in their specific interest area.

Similarly, career academies have emerged as a way to blend technical skills, career exploration, and academics into the curriculum through small learning communities and formal partnerships with employers that provide connections to the workplace. Research shows positive relationships between students and teachers in career academies, as well as a positive connection between students' academic achievement and career prospects. These findings are especially pronounced for students who are classified at medium or high risk of dropping out (Kemple, 2004). However, Kemple (2004; Kemple and Willner, 2008) did not find that students from career academies were more likely than control group students to attain a high school diploma or college degree.

Small Learning Environments

Beyond their effects on college goals and academic rigor, microsystems affect the individual level of support that students experience, the information they receive, and what Knight-Diop (2010) terms the "interpersonal structures of care" that students experience (p. 171). Small schools, houses, and learning communities group small numbers of students with teachers to provide environments where individuals have a greater likelihood of forming strong relationships with mentors (Levine, 2002; Shear and others, 2005; Wasley and others, 2000). Adults who know students well can elicit academic engagement and tailor recommendations and assignments to students' developmental needs and specific subject area interests (Conley, 2010; Knight-Diop, 2010; Quint, Thompson, and Bald, 2008). Small learning environments are most effective when students receive high-quality instruction, advising, and expectations. As Antrop-Gonzalez and De Jesus (2006) reiterate, the "relevance and quality of instruction and the interpersonal relations that form inside these [smaller learning communities] is far more significant than their size" (p. 410).

Teacher-Student Relationships

Within schools, teachers play a central role in preparing students for college. Students can distinguish teachers whom they perceive care about them and want them to succeed academically and personally. There is great variability in teachers' willingness and ability to counsel students through the college admissions process. Student-teacher interactions may also differ by student, class level, and school. Although students frequently talk to teachers about college (Venezia and Kirst, 2005), not all teachers see college conversations and advising as their responsibility (Perna, Rowan-Kenyon, Thomas, and Bell, 2008). Nor do teachers always have correct information to give students (Venezia and Kirst, 2005). Based on focus groups with teachers in California, Immerwahr (2003) found that teachers in low-income schools can be frustrated and overwhelmed by a sense of powerlessness in the face of students' individual problems, leading them to be unintentionally unsupportive of students. Some research has found that Latino high school students perceive teachers to have lower expectations of them than of their white and black peers (Cheng and Starks, 2002).

School Counselors

Within the school, counselors are another potential microsystem for students. Ideally, counselors provide useful guidance and advice to students and intervene effectively to resolve problems. In a study of nationally recognized exemplary schools, researchers found that effective counselors promote the integration of college knowledge into the school experience through activities such as field trips to colleges or conversations about college applications in class (Militello and others, 2009).

Through their leadership in the school, counselors serve as a potential avenue for the communication of high college expectations to students and families. However, the ratio of counselors to students can reach as high as five hundred students to one counselor. Furthermore, many counselors report that they did not receive adequate training to assist students and families in areas related to college readiness (Savitz-Romer, 2012). Multiple roles can also reduce counselors' influence on students by constraining their ability to provide sufficient advising about appropriate course work, graduation requirements, and the college application process (Fitch and Marshall, 2004; Militello and others, 2009). In light of such high student loads and role demands, Rueda (2005) concluded that infrequent contact with students was the cause of counselors' negligible influence on most students' college preparation. There is some indication, however, that the counselor-student relationship deepens later in the high school years (Bell, Rowan-Kenyon, and Perna, 2009).

Problems arise when students who need counseling often fail to realize the persistence and active outreach they need to undertake to initiate contact with the underresourced counselors (Perna, Rowan-Kenyon, Thomas, and Bell, 2008). Problems also arise in the differential types of advice students in low- and high-resourced schools receive in the college choice process (Bryan, Holcomb-McCoy, Moore-Thomas, and Day-Vines, 2009; Perna, Rowan-Kenyon, Thomas, and Bell, 2008).

Out-of-School Microsystems

Numerous settings and roles that occupy students' immediate environment can overlap with school or reside completely beyond the school environment. Although the field of youth development focuses on community microsystems, including workplace, neighborhoods, social services, and congregations (Benson, Scales, Hamilton, and Sesma, 2006; Gambone, Klem, and Connell, 2002), this work is largely absent from the college readiness literature. Rather, a great deal of literature centers on the influence that preparation programs, families, and peers have on preparing individuals for college and increasing college aspirations (Deil-Amen and Turley, 2007; Immerwahr, 2003).

Preparation Programs

In addition to schools, college readiness programs occupy a significant place in participants' lives, playing a pivotal role in supporting in-school microsystems and compensating for schools' shortcomings in preparing students for college. College readiness programs typically have particular areas of focus, such as providing test preparation, science and math preparation, counseling, academics, college information, and motivational and social development (Schultz and Mueller, 2006; Tierney and Garcia, 2011; Tierney and Jun, 2001). Most commonly, programs focus on raising awareness of college and developing students' social skills (Swail, 2000; Swail and Perna, 2000). Some of the best-known and most extensively evaluated programs include Advancement Via Individual Determination (AVID); GEAR UP; Puente; Upward Bound; and Mathematics, Engineering, and Science Achievement (MESA).

As Table 2 displays, the evaluation and research literature includes extensive discussion of effective practices in college readiness programs. There is considerable consensus across school and program studies about best practices in supporting student academic preparation, college knowledge, and college entrance tasks. Overall, there is strong agreement that programs are most effective in developing college readiness when they provide comprehensive services to students, including academic support, and when student involvement is sustained over an extended period of time.

Evaluators and researchers have provided detailed descriptions and studies of major college readiness programs that reflect principles listed in Table 2. In the federally funded Upward Bound program, for example, the majority of students enter as ninth or tenth graders and are low income or first generation to attend college, or both. Students participate in academic, cultural, and college-knowledge programming on a semiweekly basis and academic programming during summers. They receive tutoring, counseling, and tailored instruction. Upward Bound has been found to have positive effects on postsecondary achievement for certain subgroups, such as students who applied for admission to Upward Bound in tenth grade or later and those with a 2.5 GPA or higher in ninth grade (Seftor, Mamun, and Schirm, 2009).

TABLE 2

Effective practices in college preparation and outreach programs

Practice	Description
Provide Academic Support	Embed the preparation program in K–12 schools such that it is aligned with course work and provides seamless support.
	Focus on providing high-quality academic support that supplements students' school curriculum.
Offer Holistic Supports	Offer comprehensive, multifaceted interventions.
	Provide social support.
	Offer financial support and incentives, such as support for the SAT.
	Assist students through the admissions process.
Provide Personalized Attention and Supports	Provide culturally sensitive programming and staffing.
	Tailor attention and services to students' individual needs.
Time Supports Strategically	Implement interventions during critical time periods during the college admissions and preparation process.
	Provide college transition counseling in the summer after high school graduation
	Offer long-term support.
Build a Network of Supporters	Draw on peers to offer social support and foster students' aspirations.
	Draw on adults to serve as role models.
Keep It Relevant to Community and Careers	Connect programming to the community.
	Connect programming to careers.
	Involve families in the learning process.
Foster College Aspirations and Support Application	Help students understand that college is an option, their range of college options, and how to pay.
	Be persistent in providing messages to students about the possibility of going to college.

Sources: Castleman, Arnold, and Wartman (2012); Engle, Bermeo, and O'Brien, 2006; Gandara and Bial (2001); Gullat and Jan (2003); Hayward, Brandes, Kirst, and Mazzeo (1997); Schultz and Mueller (2006); Tierney and Hagedorn (2007).

Gullatt and Jan (2003) describe how another program, Baltimore College Bound, embodies research-based core principles of effective outreach programs by providing high standards for students, personalized attention, role models, peer support, integration into the K–12 setting, a long-term approach, and financial aid support. Students hear presentations about college as ninth and tenth graders and later receive assistance in filling out application forms. The program also provides students with funds to bridge the gap between financial aid awards and college tuition costs. Based on a series of program evaluations, Gullat and Jan (2003) found that Baltimore College Bound participants were more likely to attend and persist in college.

Preparation programs have been found to have significant positive effects on students' academic performance in college (Gandara, 2002; Watt, Huerta and Lozano, 2007; Winkleby and others, 2009). For example, Watt, Huerta, and Lozano (2007) found that AVID has a positive effect on advanced college course taking when compared to control group and other college prep programs. They also found that AVID and GEAR UP students had higher college knowledge and aspirations than a control group (Lozano, Watt, and Huerta, 2009). However, with few rigorous evaluations with control groups, knowledge about the impact of college preparation programs is incomplete.

Families

A substantial body of literature points to the importance of family support and encouragement of academic achievement behaviors and educational aspirations (Fan and Chen, 2001; Hill and others, 2004; Jeynes, 2003; Tierney and Auerbach, 2005). Parents are especially important in guiding their children's aspirations and discussing college plans in the early high school years. Parents can take responsibility for setting expectations for their students, including urging their sons and daughters not to follow their examples if they themselves did not attend college (Yamamura, Martinez, and Saenz, 2010). Parents can also play an active role in seeking out information and saving for college (Cabrera and La Nasa, 2000).

It is well established that family socioeconomic status is related to children's subsequent education level (Crosnoe, 2001; McDonough, 1997;

Walpole, 2003). High school graduates are substantially less likely to be qualified to attend college if their parents have not attended college (49 percent) compared to graduates with at least one parent with a degree (15 percent) (Choy, 2001). Children of noncollege-educated parents are also less likely to take advanced mathematics in high school (63 percent) compared to graduates whose parents had a bachelor's degree (Choy, 2001). In their review of literature of student success, Perna and Thomas (2008) point to research that shows students' academic achievement is intertwined with parents' ethnicity and educational attainment and job security.

Children must make decisions about their own education when the family lacks knowledge about higher education and pathways to college (Immerwahr, 2003). For instance, in examining a group of Latino "college maybes" or high schoolers who were unsure whether they would enroll in college, Immerwahr (2003) found that many of these youth had little adult guidance. Although Latino parents have been found to value college highly as a path to their children's success (Immerwahr, 2003), inequities in college knowledge persist. Researchers have identified lower levels of college knowledge among low-income black and Latino families in comparison to white and Asian families (Rowan-Kenyon, Bell, and Perna, 2008; Tornatzky, Cutler, and Lee, 2002). Language barriers also stand as a major impediment to college knowledge (Tornatzky, Cutler, and Lee, 2002), an important factor in explaining the poor college knowledge of Latino parents who are not fluent English speakers.

Peers

Second only to parents, peers play a particularly large role in college readiness and are highly influential during the developmental period that coincides with the traditional high school years (Sokatch, 2006). The peers with whom students most frequently come into contact strongly affect school success (Coleman and others, 1966; Crosnoe, 2000). Although these effects are uneven (Tierney and Colyar, 2005), peers are an important part of students' lives and can be used as a strategic tool to increase college enrollment (Hossler, Schmit, and Vesper, 1999) and for support in academic preparation (Gullatt and Jan, 2003). Peers share information about college going (Bell, Rowan-Kenyon, and Perna, 2009; Stanton-Salazar, 2004; Tierney and Venegas, 2007;

Yamamura, Martinez, and Saenz, 2010). Within the school, peers mediate students' use of resources and school experiences (Knight-Diop, 2010). For instance, friends affect the classes students choose, including the selection of college preparatory courses (Wimberly and Noeth, 2005). However, peer effects vary across different groups, with Latinos and black students having less peer-based support for their achievement (Steinberg, Dornsbusch, and Brown, 1992) and some peer groups of color collectively resisting academic achievement (Fordham and Ogbu, 1986; Ogbu, 1978).

Cocurricular Activities

Individuals also participate in activities outside the classroom, such as sports teams, clubs, or other youth groups. In their review of the effects of cocurricular activities on college preparation, Hearn and Holdsworth (2005) found some positive relationships between cocurricular participation and students' self-efficacy, self-esteem, social skill development, academic achievement, and aspirations. Some research has connected participation in formal school cocurricular activities with higher grades and test scores (Broh, 2002), particularly for nonathletic activities (Guest and Schneider, 2003). Although effects vary by extracurricular activity and subgroup, on the whole the focus of literature is on school-related extracurricular activities (Hearn and Holdsworth, 2005).

Social Media and the Internet

Social media and the Internet reach students both inside and outside school settings and serve as microsystems that can enhance students' academic preparation and college knowledge. Nine in ten U.S. teenagers (93 percent) age twelve to seventeen go online, and a substantial proportion of those teenagers obtain news about current events (62 percent) and health information (31 percent) online (Lenhart, Purcell, Smith, and Zickuhr, 2010).

Increasingly, Web-based college readiness applications are reaching students on sites they most frequently visit. For example, the University of Southern California's Facebook-based game invites individuals to learn the rules of the college admissions process through a simulated experience. Colleges are turning toward private Facebook applications, like Inigral's

Schools App, to connect accepted students with school activities and other students while monitoring their patterns of engagement. Other Web-based portals such as Naviance assist students, teachers, parents, and counselors in topics that range from individual students' college choice process to housing information about students' high school grades and course work and identifying potential colleges for students based on their interests and academic background. Although the literature in this area is nascent, the Internet and social media serve as promising microsystems that can reinforce students' college and content knowledge in out-of-school environments in which young people are deeply immersed.

Direct Experience in an Ecological Context

Among school, family, friends, and out-of-school commitments, students traverse distinct worlds on a daily basis. Each of these environments provides varying opportunities to develop college readiness (Kimura-Walsh, Yamamura, Griffin, and Allen, 2009; Padilla, 2009b; Perna, 2006). Microsystems serve as crucial sites in the college preparation process, setting different norms, roles, and opportunities that advance students' college readiness (Rueda, 2005). Yet not all microsystems are congruent or resource rich. Organizations and policy influences emanating from the exosystem shape the availability and content of school and community settings. One resource-enriched environment can help offset the deficits or negative drawbacks of others. Conversely, in other cases, students may gravitate toward microsystems that inhibit the development of college readiness. As the following chapters detail, microsystems exist within other levels of the environment that affect them. To make progress in college readiness among economically and educationally challenged students, policymakers, teachers, program staff, and families must move across and beyond microsystems.

Mesosystem: A Network of Overlapping Relationships

THE DEVELOPMENT OF COLLEGE READINESS occurs in the immediate settings of a student's life, but each individual microsystem is only a part of that student's total experience. Higher education aspirations and college readiness are affected by the intersecting orbits in which students are simultaneously involved. The mesosystem is the totality of students' direct experiences, roles, and settings—the combined set of microsystem interactions. Intervention in any single setting must take into account the interactions across them. For low-income and first-generation students, mixed messages and different actors across roles and settings often add up to a fragmented, incongruent mesosystem. This lack of alignment is in vivid contrast to the experience of middle-class students for whom expectations, knowledge, and experience consistently point to higher education (Arnold and others, 2009). The research on college readiness touches on mesosystem factors primarily in the areas of cultural and social capital, family involvement in schools and programs, and simultaneous student enrollment in high school and college.

Cultural Capital and the Mesosystem

Cultural approaches to college preparation and access map onto the intersecting set of immediate environments and roles that make up the mesosystem. Cultural capital explanations of educational stratification point to the ways in which informal knowledge, personal tastes, attitudes and values, and styles of self-presentation are shaped within systems of power relations in the greater society (Bourdieu, 1967, 1977, 1986; Bourdieu and Passeron, 1977; McDonough, 1997; Winkle-Wagner, 2010). Students who come from low-income or ethnic minority backgrounds, this framework suggests, are disadvantaged in formal educational settings in which the cultural knowledge and forms of expression of dominant social groups determine expectations and rewards.

Cultural capital analyses of college readiness can be viewed in terms of mesosystem interactions in which students simultaneously navigate home and school environments that call for different understandings and behaviors (Tierney and Garcia, 2011). Bridging the different norms and tacit knowledge of higher education and low-income communities of color is the major barrier to college access featured in mesosystem approaches. Students can also encounter capital-based incongruence within high schools, as middle-class guidance counselors assume that low-income students and families share their assumptions and knowledge about higher education (McDonough, 1997). These cross-setting mismatches in cultural capital—not any deficit in individuals—result in marginalization and associated academic disengagement for low-income students (Koyama, 2007).

William Tierney and colleagues (Tierney and Hagedorn 2007; Tierney and Jun, 2001; Tierney and Venegas, 2009) have broadened the lens of culture to provide the closest equivalent to a mesosystem framework in the literature to date. As these researchers highlight, students are simultaneously part of families, peer groups, neighborhoods, communities, and schools, settings that are connected and dynamic. Students are affected by particular environments and interactions among those environments. Environmental influences include multiple messages about college, "even if those inputs are nonexistent or negative" (Tierney and Venegas, 2009, p. 383). Importantly, students also shape individual environments and environmental interactions as they make decisions that both reflect and rebuild their mesosystem. A cultural integrity framework for college preparation programs calls for connecting the contexts of students' lives by treating cultural traits as strengths that can be incorporated as positive resources for learning (Jun and Colyar, 2002; Jun and Tierney, 1999).

Villalpando and Solorzano (2005) reviewed research on the inclusion of culture in college preparation programs. According to their analysis, some readiness programs attempt to minimize mixed messages—mesosystem incongruity—by trying to help students deemphasize or even leave their home culture and communities. Other programs seek to harmonize dissimilar cultures by highlighting, valuing, and incorporating participants' culture. A cultural wealth perspective (Solorzano and Villalpando, 1998) attempts to understand and make use of culturally specific activities, beliefs, norms, and structures that are compatible with educational achievement. Similarly, college preparation programs can draw from communities for mentors and role models that affirm students' culture and reduce the perception that school success means rejecting one's own background (Oesterreich, 2000).

Social Capital and Mesosystem Connectors

In addition to economic and cultural capital, students draw on social resources to shape their expectations and carry out their plans for higher education. Social capital consists of strong and weak ties to others that make up an individual's social networks (Lin, 2001). The role of parents makes up most of the research on social capital and higher education. Most of this research situates family as a key microsystem for students. *Family engagement* typically refers to college information, encouragement, and assistance within the family. Evidence of incongruence between college-going messages and behaviors in the family, as opposed to those in school and college preparation programs, is a staple of research (Bell, Rowan-Kenyon and Perna, 2009; Smith, 2008). These studies emphasize the relations across individual microsystems.

Ecological theory goes beyond this approach to focus attention on the ways in which microsystems overlap through common membership. Direct family connections with schools and college preparation programs are the leading example of this type of research. Tierney and Auerbach (2005) note that the definitions of *family engagement* and *family involvement* are unclear and inconsistent in the literature. These terms are used to refer to a variety of behaviors, mostly occurring within the family system. For instance, parental encouragement of students' college aspirations or support of academic achievement behaviors takes place in the microsystem of the family. Even these positive behaviors within the family setting are insufficient to guarantee academic achievement and college planning behaviors. Direct connections between family and other key settings are needed. The importance of overlapping systems is underlined by the findings of a large report that found that the only family factor that made a difference in college access was the parent accompanying his or her child on a campus visit (Bedsworth, Colby, and Doctor, 2006).

When *involvement* is taken to mean family members' direct experience within a student microsystem, mesosystem interactions refer to parents' presence in schools and college preparation programs. Parents are involved in schools when they communicate with teachers and counselors, volunteer in the schools, or participate in school activities like college nights or financial aid workshops (Epstein, 1990, 1995). Similarly, families can be directly involved in college preparation programs. Parents who intervene with school or college program staff on behalf of their child create mesosystem interactions. In comparison to the self-efficacy and sense of entitlement of privileged "helicopter parents," low-income parents are less likely to possess the cultural norms, tacit understandings, and self-efficacy to intervene in school (Tierney and Auerbach, 2005; Wartman and Savage, 2008).

In their excellent review of the role of families in college preparation, Tierney and Auerbach (2005) note that this part of the literature is not well developed: "We still do not know enough about how diverse families interact with schools and precisely what type and degree of parent engagement is most efficacious for certain students under particular conditions" (p. 31). As in their cultural analysis of college preparation, Tierney and Auerbach draw attention to ethnic and socioeconomic differences that affect the ways in which schools and researchers define and evaluate family involvement (Tierney and Auerbach, 2005; Jun and Colyar, 2002). Involving parents in schools and college preparation programs is a consistent theme in the college access literature (Venezia, Kirst, and Antonio, 2002; Wimberly and Noeth, 2005). Success in involving parents is increased by aligning cultural norms and practices across the microsettings of school, preparation programs, and family and community (Tierney and Auerbach, 2005).

Despite widespread agreement on the positive effects of parent involvement, schools and college programs struggle to incorporate families. For instance, high school counselors believe that they should work with parents about college opportunities but do relatively little of this work (Bridgeland and Bruce, 2011; Holcomb-McCoy, 2010). In contrast, one study of award-winning high schools found that counselors aggressively reached out to low-income parents with services and programs that were compatible with parents' logistical, cultural, and language contexts (Militello and others, 2009). As an element of broader educational reform, parental involvement requires an overall school climate that families find welcoming and inviting (Holcomb-McCoy, 2010).

Reviews of college preparation programs vary in their estimate of mandatory parental involvement, from 22 to 25 percent of programs (Swail, 2000; Tierney and Auerbach, 2005) to 50 percent (Gandara and Bial, 2001). In a survey of over eleven hundred programs between 1999 and 2000, the National Survey of Outreach Programs found that approximately two-thirds of all programs included a parental component (Perna and Swail, 2001; Swail, 2000). In many of these cases, however, the parental component signified only that parents were asked to sign participation agreements for their student. Rueda (2005) concludes that "few programs include a family component, and when families are included it is often in a trivial fashion" (p. 192). Despite problems in implementation, researchers call for continued efforts to involve parents in college readiness programs (Myers and Myers, 2012; Oesterreich, 2000; Swail and Perna, 2002; Tierney and Auerbach, 2005).

A student's social capital includes ties beyond parents. In fact, in low-income families, parents' involvement in their children's educational activities tends to decline as students move through middle school and high school (Bell, Rowan-Kenyan, and Perna, 2009; Wimberly and Noeth, 2005). But other important people in a student's life can connect settings through meso-system interactions. Older siblings and relatives, school teachers and counselors, college program staff, and community mentors are all potential connectors across student microsystems (Bell, Rowan-Kenyon, and Perna, 2009; Gandara, 1995; McDonough, 1997). Friends and other peers affect students' course-taking choices, educational aspirations, and academic behaviors (Wimberly and Noeth, 2005).

Connectors who link students across school, programs, and nonschool contexts can bring isolated microsystems into overlapping, congruent mesosystem interactions. School counselors are positioned to collaborate with school, family, and community members to bring together resources, information, and support for students. Cultural and linguistic links are important in realizing the potential of counselors as mesosystem connectors (Tornatzky, Cutler, and Lee, 2002). College student tutors bring the postsecondary world into the direct experience of precollege students (Hayward, Brandes, Kirst, and Mazzeo, 1997). Relationships between students and adults in college preparation programs are particularly well suited to bridging students' otherwise separate worlds of home, community, and school (Hayward, Brandes, Kirst, and Mazzeo, 1997). Program advisers serve as institutional agents (Moreno, 2002) and mediators of knowledge across cultures (Rueda, Monzó, and Arzubiaga, 2003). Ideally students develop a close personal relationship in schools and programs with at least one adult who "mediates the relationship between families, high schools, and colleges" (Hayward, Brandes, Kirst, and Mazzeo, 1997, p. 20). Community members who serve as mentors and role models provide students with mesosystem interactions in which students enter settings where college attendance is normative (McGrath, Swisher, Elder, and Conger, 2001; Oesterreich, 2000). Connections to jobs and employers in the workplace are another mesosystem interaction provided by community-based organizations that draw on youth development principles to motivate students and prepare them for postsecondary success (American Youth Policy Forum, 1997).

Research on college outreach programs supports the advantages of connecting settings through direct experience in overlapping contexts. In their comprehensive review of college preparation programs, Hayward, Brandes, Kirst, and Mazzeo conclude that the most effective outreach programs are "well-integrated with K–12 schools instead of operating at the margins" (1997, p. 25). In a negative example of the same principle, college outreach information campaigns are generally ineffective partly because they fail to engage "those who influence [students'] decision-making (community organizations and leaders, parents, coaches, adults who serve as informal mentors, etc.)" (Pathways to College Network, 2002, paragraph 3) or embed their messages in the media of youth culture. Programs such as Puente, AVID, and the Neighborhood Academic Initiative that explicitly connect students' cultural contexts to college preparation activities do so in part by facilitating overlap between student microsystems (Bergerson, 2009; Gandara, 2002; Gandara and Mejorado, 2005; Moreno, 2002; Rendon, 2002; Villalpando and Solorzano, 2005).

College and High School Integration

A mesosystem lens on college readiness reveals that low-income students generally encounter isolated and misaligned college understandings and preparation behaviors across their immediate environments of school, family, community, and peers. Learning about higher education or following a college-preparatory curriculum is not equivalent to direct experience with college. Promising curricular alignment efforts like Advanced Placement and International Baccalaureate programs still place college outside the high school student's set of microsystems (Hallett and Venegas, 2011; Perna and others, 2011; Scott, Tolson, and Lee, 2010). Even when a particular microsystem stresses high educational aspirations and academic success, students' overall experience frequently falls short of the sustained, complex repertoire of knowledge and behaviors required for college access and success.

Mesosystem interactions involving a student in both high school and higher education settings go beyond information and preparation for college within precollege settings. The most straightforward direct overlap between high school and college is the presence of high school students on college campuses. Campus visits by precollege students appear to make a positive difference in college access for low-income students (Beasley-Wojick, Braggs, and Schneider, 2011; Bedsworth, Colby, and Doctor, 2006; Hayward, Brandes, Kirst, and Mazzeo, 1997). Promising results have also been reported from the campus visit component of a Hartford, Connecticut, college preparation program for low-income fifth and ninth graders (Druckman, 2007). In the Hartford study, the direct experience of an extensive on-campus experience was a motivator to students to remain in college-preparatory courses across critical school transitions.

Approximately half of the eleven hundred college preparation programs in the National Survey of Outreach Programs were found to take place on a college or university campus (Swail, 2000). An earlier study found that at least one-third of all higher education institutions had at least one outreach program (NCES, 1996, cited in Swail, 2000). College student tutors are a mainstay of such programs, providing a direct link to the college regardless of the location where they work with students.

Although campus-based outreach programs and college-based program staff place higher education within a student's mesosystem, these programs are rarely sustained and comprehensive enough to make a critical difference in college access and success. For instance, evaluators studying the outcomes of the federal Upward Bound program found that participation in the program had no overall effect on higher education enrollment, degree attainment, application for financial aid, or Pell grant receipt (Seftor, Mamun, and Schirm, 2009). Longer participation in the program was associated with increased higher education matriculation and degree completion, however, lending empirical support to the positive effects of sustained participation in college outreach programs.

Educational arrangements that involve students in simultaneous, overlapping high school and college settings attempt to provide comprehensive mesosystem interventions. The Neighborhood Academic Initiative program in California, for instance, brings middle school and high school students to the University of Southern California campus for an intensive academic program that occurs over multiple years and includes teachers and tutors from the home school and the university. The campus location and staff enable precollege students to "feel they belong and also get a sense of what going to college means" (Tierney and Jun, 2001, p. 217).

Efforts to link high school and postsecondary institutions go back at least a hundred years, including calls for a movement in the 1930s and 1940s to connect the last two years of secondary school with the first two years of higher education (Kisker, 2006). Various dual-enrollment programs, including those aimed at disengaged high school students or previous dropouts, enable students to take college classes before graduating from high school (Steinberg and Allen, 2011). Two-year colleges have always been at the center of these partnerships, as in the case of the middle college high school movement that began in the 1970s (Lieberman, 1988; Wechsler, 2001). Located on community college campuses, middle college high schools enroll low-income students in programs designed to integrate high school and community college course work. Despite the positive effects of middle college high schools on graduates' postsecondary enrollment and degree attainment, governance and funding challenges have prevented the model from spreading widely or attaining genuine integration of high school and community college education (Kisker, 2006).

Early college high schools are the current manifestation of repeated efforts to integrate high school and college experiences in students' mesosystem for economically and educationally challenged students. Unlike middle college high schools, early college high schools have an explicit goal for students to attain significant college credit before high school graduation. The Early College High School Initiative involves students in a four-year blend of high school and college work that allows them simultaneously to earn a high school diploma and one to two years of tuition-free, transferable college credit (Allen and Murphy, 2008; Le and Frankfort, 2011). Sponsored by the Bill and Melinda Gates Foundation and several other foundations, the Early College High School Initiative is coordinated and evaluated by the nonprofit Jobs for the Future organization and carried out by a wide array of intermediary partners. The project began in 2001, and the first early college high schools opened in 2002. At the ten-year mark, 270 new or redesigned early college high schools had collectively served more than seventy-five thousand students in twenty-eight states (Le and Frankfort, 2011). Most of the schools are located on or near a community college campus (Kisker, 2006).

Early college high schools share common goals but also vary along key dimensions that affect how students experience the connection between high school and college. Common distinguishers of the model include small size, personalization, and individualized academic and social support for students. Each school has a postsecondary partner, typically a community college, and each attempts to integrate students' high school and college experience through a single, coherent cross-institution academic program. Every early college high school provides a course of study in which students can earn as much as sixty college credits while still in high school (Hoffman and Vargas, 2010). The amount of integration between the college and high school varies, according to an analysis of design elements by Allen and Murphy (2008). Less intensive partnerships focus on "better signaling" in the form of elements such as college student tutoring and campus visits. Moderate levels of intervention "blur boundaries" between high school and college by having college faculty teach in the high school and sending high school students to the college campus for after-school and summer work and recreation. The most intensive models "blend" high school and community college with practices such as college skills courses, dual-credit courses, team teaching with high school and college faculty, carefully aligned and scaffolded curricula, and cross-institution advising and academic support (Allen and Murphy, 2008).

Proponents of the early college high school model point to increased student motivation and achievement resulting from high school structures that align the curriculum and entry to college, provide college success support, and compress the time and money required to earn an associate's degree. Early results from the Early College High School Initiative are promising in terms of increased high school graduation, direct college enrollment, and four-year college enrollment, according to analyses of students who graduated from initiative schools between 2006 and 2009 (Le and Frankfort, 2011; Nodine, 2009; Vargas and Miller, 2011). From an ecological perspective, this model of partnership between high school and college represents a genuine mesosystem intervention that has great potential for systemic change in the entire developmental ecology of underrepresented students. The early college movement is still new, however, and college persistence data are not yet available.

Overlapping Relationships in the Ecological Context

A mesosystem theoretical lens suggests that the disappointing findings about overall program and policy effects might arise from the failure to account for the multiple intersections across schools, programs, family, and friends. Tierney and Venegas (2009) come closest to proposing a mesosystem model of conceiving an overall environment of multiple microsystems. Noting that students and their families make decisions within relational contexts, Tierney and Venegas (2009) characterize the social environment as connected, dynamic, interacting systems that both operate on students and are affected by students. Above all, a mesosystem emphasis argues for comprehensive college readiness activities that touch all aspects of students' lives.

Connections among settings and roles are affected by other parts of the human ecosystem. A student's developmentally instigative and demographic characteristics affect the ways in which the messages and demands of multiple microsystems collectively influence his or her college readiness. Students' roles such as employee, sibling caregiver, or family translator also shape the meeting points across their direct settings. The quality of individual microsystems clearly influences the mesosystem. Finally, students might experience multiple roles and settings as dissonant or overwhelming because of larger forces beyond their immediate environments. Policies, organizational practices, history, culture, and ideology shape the ways in which students experience the totality of their daily lives.

Exosystem: The Site of Systemic and Structural Changes

THE EARLIER CHAPTERS DESCRIBING the micro- and mesosystems explore how immediate environments and their connections affect the lives of individual students. Also explored are the interaction of these systems with each other and the various effects on individual students as they make their way toward college. An ecological model of college readiness proposes that all aspects of students' lives, the factors in their surrounding environment, and the systems in place to support these elements must be considered to understand fully what is needed for college readiness. Moving to the next level in this model, the exosystem serves as a lens to view the effect of the larger environment on students' access to college.

In Bronfenbrenner's theory, the exosystem refers to influences on the individual that are not part of the student's immediate setting, including organizations and structures in which the student is not physically present but indirectly influence his or her immediate environments. Exosystem factors include government, foundations, and other policymaking settings, as well as organizational structures, norms, laws, regulations, and educational or labor force credentialing systems (Bronfenbrenner, 1979). In the world of college readiness for students, these emanate from different sources and can influence the individual student at different points in time or simultaneously exert multiple influences on a student's experience. Intervention program design and curriculum reform, for example, can occur at the school or district level, or both, of a student's community. Accountability efforts and policies affecting financial aid and tuition funding occur at the state and the federal levels, as well as at higher education institutions. All of these factors can influence the experience of individual students and manifest as a change to the curriculum, a required assessment for graduation, a change in access to financial aid, or the experience of taking a challenging standardized college entry test. Although students are not personally involved with a statewide standards movement or a new merit-based college grant program, these exosystem influences from the larger environment have deep effects on students' ability to become college ready (Renn and Arnold, 2003).

The literature describing exosystem-level organizations and policies created to increase college readiness and access is wide reaching. It ranges from examinations of types of programs to analyses of the effect of policies instituted by larger entities such as school systems, state boards, and the federal government. A review of the exosystem and its complexity requires a consideration of the various categories of influences that contribute to the students' ecological environment.

The first category of influences includes policies and programs designed to support early intervention and school reform efforts, such as the restructuring of the K–12 curriculum (Roderick, Nagaoka, and Coca, 2009; Steinberg, Almeida, Allen, and Goldberger, 2003). Other intervention efforts focus on policies instituted at various stages in students' development, such as the middle school years (Perna and Swail, 2001). Still others focus on reforms through collaborative high school and college partnerships designed to move students toward college sooner than the traditional time frame (Pennington, 2004).

The arena of readiness program design is part of students' exosystem because students are affected by the decisions educators and administrators make about how programs are conceptualized and delivered but are excluded from decision making. Research in this area examines the wide variety of college readiness programs that have been created since 1970. For large long-standing programs, such as GEAR UP and College Bound, some research examines the program's signature elements and participant outcomes (Watt, Huerta, and Lozano, 2007). Other researchers look across different programs for those characteristics that prove to be critical toward success (Pathways to College Network, 2002; Swail, 2004; Tierney and Hagedorn, 2007). The broadest approaches arrive from researchers proposing new program designs of best practice and evaluation based on successful characteristics gleaned from research across various programs (Hayward, Brandes, Kirst, and Mazzeo, 1997; Kazis, Pennington, and Conklin, 2003; Lumina Foundation, 2009; Perna, 2006).

A second category found in the policy literature addresses efforts sponsored by the states and federal government, including school-to-college programs focused on K–16 alignment (Kazis, Pennington, and Conklin, 2003; Walsh, 2004). A body of literature argues that when the K–12 curriculum is not coordinated or aligned, with requirements and expectations at the college level, students are not prepared for a successful college experience (Walsh, 2004). When alignment issues appear on the federal level, they often take the form of policies addressing the dissemination of financial aid or the implementation of common standards and accountability methods (Haskins and Kemple, 2009). Large foundations and private organizations, such as the Bill and Melinda Gates Foundation, also play a role in the support of intervention and reform efforts, with increasing numbers of partnerships between private organizations and government (Kazis, 2006).

An examination of the varied approaches to policymaking and systemic reform to improve college readiness shows that many of the large programs and reform efforts are wide reaching and can demonstrate a number of successful outcomes for participating students. In light of the ecological model, however, they typically lack a comprehensive view of the environments that make an impact on a student's successful approach to college readiness. Even within the exosystem, the many layers of organizations may not connect effectively or in a coordinated way with one another. School district policies on curriculum reform, for example, often fail to mirror the entrance requirements for the state college system. Federal financial aid policies do not typically reflect an understanding of the barriers that English language learners face (Tierney and Venegas, 2009).

The exosystem is complicated by the diverse number of organizational leaders and policymakers attempting to improve college readiness and access from their various perspectives (Pasque, 2007). Reform efforts exist at the school, district, state, and federal government levels. Sources of funding for these reforms also can vary widely, often through combinations of these various levels. From the perspective of the ecological model, the individual student indirectly experiences the influences of all these factors as a consequence of how policies have affected the development of educational intervention programs or through the impact of school reform on the classroom environment. Policies that are crafted at the state and federal levels also play a large role in individual students' lives by their ability to increase access through K–16 alignment or the distribution of financial aid (St. John, 2006, 2007).

An overview of the general categories of reform, along with salient examples from research, demonstrates the various influences on students and highlights the gaps between policies and proximal processes of development in the immediate experience of economically and educationally challenged students.

Precollege Intervention Programs

There are thousands of precollege intervention programs in existence, and many of their characteristics and effects on individual students were described in the "Microsystem" chapter. The creation and design of college preparation programs, and how they are sponsored and supported, are a function of the influences of the larger community surrounding students and the policies that affect a particular environment.

In 2000, the College Board conducted the National Survey of Outreach Programs and collected data from eleven hundred programs (Swail, 2000). Although these programs were widely varied in their approaches and methods, all were designed to help economically and educationally challenged students prepare and navigate toward higher education. Programs also targeted different levels of the school pipeline, including the middle school years. College preparation programs were sponsored by all levels of a student's community, originating with local, state, or federal agencies; private organizations or foundations; and colleges and universities (Perna, Fenske, and Swail, 2000).

The federal government has supported intervention programs since the 1960s. Most notable of these is the collection of TRIO programs, which consists of Talent Search, Upward Bound, and Student Support Services. Upward Bound sponsors extensive academic and counseling support, while Talent Search provides information regarding admissions and financial aid to students and families and also encourages high school graduation and enrollment in postsecondary institutions. The Student Support Services program within TRIO provides academic support to students at the higher education level (McElroy and Armesto, 1998).

The federal government also has partnered with state and local governments in the creation and sponsorship of intervention programs. One of the first collaborations as part of the reauthorization of the Higher Education Act, the 1992 National Early Intervention and Scholarship and Partnership (NEISP), provided matching funds to states for intervention programs. In 1998, the next reauthorization of the Higher Education Act transformed the NEISP program into Gaining Early Awareness and Readiness for Undergraduate Programs (GEAR UP) with the goal of increasing enrollments among low-income students by identifying a particular cohort within a low-income school and requiring partnerships with local colleges, community organizations, and schools. Other national school reform initiatives, such as Project Graduation Really Achieves Dreams, are designed to improve academic achievement by intervening throughout an integrated K–12 system (Snipes, Holton, Doolittle, and Sztejnberg, 2006).

School and college partnerships became prevalent in the 1970s and 1980s, typically consisting of out-of-school enrichment activities, navigation skills for admissions, mentoring, tutoring, and summer enrichment or college preparatory programs. Federal and state governments sponsor these programs through organizations such as the Education Trust and the State Higher Education Executive Officers. In addition, colleges and universities have developed their own early intervention and outreach programs, often with a focus on preparing students at risk for the academic rigors of college. As we described in the previous chapter, community colleges and early college high schools have offered innovative programs, such as 2+2, allowing students to earn college credit while in high school (Swail and Roth, 2000).

The difficulty with such a wide variety and multiple sources for early intervention programs is that access is not systematic or available for all students who fit the definition of eligibility. Evaluation of program elements and overall effectiveness is also varied: programs are isolated from one another and not always coordinated with the local school where the student resides (St. John, 2006).

Policymakers who design intervention programs might not have the complete picture of all the factors affecting a student's readiness for college as outlined in the ecological model. Nor do policy efforts always reach students in the ways in which they are designed (Tierney and Venegas, 2009).

School Reform

The most important setting for college readiness is the local K–12 school, but school reform, policy, and design take place in the exosystem outside the direct experience of students. Myriad studies investigate different approaches to school reform, ranging from whole school reform districtwide to smaller pilot programs in one or two schools. Reform efforts and programs are also wide ranging in their targets and approaches, from the curriculum to pedagogy, teacher quality, and school-college collaboration. All identify strategies designed to have an impact on the student's immediate learning environment and discover effective approaches for increasing college readiness. Because there are scores of examples in the literature of school reform efforts, they are described here in broad categories with salient examples to illustrate their connection with the exosystem level of the ecological model.

Many school reform efforts are inextricably linked to their source of funding at the state or federal level. Most notably, funding reforms are tied to the accountability movement in education, resulting in an increase in standards-based curricula and assessments. The school choice movement has also had an impact on the availability of resources, shifting funds to charter schools and supporting school voucher programs for private schools. College financial aid programs have been increasingly focused on academic achievement, most notably by increasing merit scholarships across districts and states (St. John, 2006).

Categories of Reform

The many examples of school reform initiatives have been described in multiple ways (Steinberg, Almeida, Allen, and Goldberger, 2003). The taxonomy described, adapted from Conley (2010), captures the major categories of reform. Similar to the earlier section on intervention programs, these efforts are too numerous to chronicle completely, but we look at a few representative types of reform.

Small Schools. The small schools movement evolved as a backlash to the large factory-style high schools created in the 1970s and the increasing student dropout rate. Small schools attempted to personalize the education experience for students by creating numerous high schools of five hundred or fewer students with the goal of challenging students toward higher achievement. They emphasize close relationships and real-world relevance in the curriculum (Conley, 2010; Levine, 2002; Raywid, 1998).

Evaluations of these models have been mixed, with some showing higher rates of college attendance yet others having difficulty achieving high rates of high school graduation. Small schools create some management issues, as they often exist on the same site as the original large high school and generate competition for common resources. Prominent examples of small school initiatives include the work of the Bill and Melinda Gates Foundation and Washington Achievers Program (Ramsey and Gorgol, 2010).

Career Academies. Structurally, career academies are high schools designed to be flexible to maximize academic learning time for students. This includes providing time for students to participate in work-based learning, which differentiates the academy model from the small school model. Career academies also provide common planning time for teachers, a critical step in restructuring schools to provide greater academic support (Martinez and Klopott, 2005). By implementing strong college preparatory curricula and expectations, career academies also provide students with crucial aid in the college planning process (Trybus and Li, 1998).

Early studies of career academies suggest that they raise academic achievement, reduce dropout rates, and increase both attendance rates and the number of credits earned toward graduation among students considered most at risk. However, they have not yet shown increased high school graduation and college enrollment rates (Kemple, 2004; Kemple and Snipes, 2000; Kemple and Willner, 2008).

Rigorous and College-Level Courses Offered in High School. An increasing number of high schools offer Advanced Placement (AP) and International Baccalaureate (IB) courses that are designed to be college-level classes taught in high schools by high school teachers. Both programs present national standards in a particular subject area. In many ways, AP courses have become the new college preparatory curriculum, because colleges value these examinations and routinely offer credit for them. The IB consists of two years' worth of specified courses in the eleventh and twelfth grades, culminating in a series of examinations and requirements calibrated against challenging college courses (Conley, 2010; Perna and others, 2011).

Widely supported by college admissions, AP and IB courses offer a combination of alignment across the school and college curriculum and an early college experience for students. Critics of the programs, however, say that the students who take them have already been in a position to achieve the top level of college course preparation (Conley, 2010). Other examples of national programs that are designed to increase course rigor include EQUITY 2000 and the Urban Systemic Initiative, which provide low-income and minority youth with increased access to rigorous curricula in mathematics and science (Martinez and Klopott, 2005).

Dual-Credit or Dual-Enrollment Programs. Policymakers have sponsored the creation of dual-credit or dual-enrollment programs in every U.S. state to allow students to enroll simultaneously in high school and in at least one college course to receive both high school and college credit. With these programs, high school students are given the chance to experience college-level expectations while still in high school. Some dual-enrollment efforts are designed specifically to increase access to higher education for minority or low-income students. The Achieving a College Education (ACE) and its sister program, ACE Plus, are designed for this purpose. ACE recruits the majority of its students as sophomores from high schools that enroll predominantly low-income, minority, and potential first-generation college students and are feeder schools for local community colleges (van Buskirk and McGrath, 1999). Similarly, College Now, in concert with the City University of New York system, offers programs that test students during their junior year of high school to determine if they are ready for credit-bearing college courses (Bailey and Karp, 2002).

Critics of dual enrollment cite issues that can arise in the mixed levels of preparation of high school students for these courses, the lack of sequencing between the courses taken in high school and those offered in college, and the varied levels of support provided by the colleges to high school students taking these courses (Conley, 2010).

Early College and Middle College High Schools. Policymakers have emphasized the importance of the creation of a cohort for students and advocated that students remain in the high school setting to receive adequate academic and social support. Early college high schools are primarily focused on college readiness and the high school–to–college transition. In these programs, secondary school students participate in college courses during their last two years while remaining enrolled in the high school. For early college high schools, typically the high school is in close partnership with a nearby community college. Middle college high schools are physically located on college campuses.

Jobs for the Future (JFF) has been a strong foundational supporter of the early college model, sharing its resources with those of other agencies, the federal government, and state collaborators (Pennington and Vargas, 2004). Other examples include the Early College High School (ECHS) program funded by several prominent foundations, including the Bill and Melinda Gates Foundation (Martinez and Klopott, 2005; Nodine, 2009).

Critics of early college, similar to the critics of dual enrollment, claim that alignment between the high schools and college courses can be a challenge, and the most successful models employ strategies to assist students in their transition to taking courses in the college environment (Conley, 2010).

School Choice. The issue of school choice and its effect on college access for students has entered the reform debate with the increase in the creation of charter schools and availability of vouchers. In this context, school choice refers to the chance for students to leave their current school and choose a new school environment. The policy implications behind the creation of these "privatized" options for students are vast, given that funding typically follows the students (St. John, 2006).

Critics of the school choice movement argue that vouchers and charters alter the flow of funding and may harm prospects for the students left behind. Charters redirect the funding of schools by allowing school dollars to follow students to new schools that are exempted from some of the educational requirements imposed on standard public schools by states and districts, while the voucher provides money for students to alter their choice from public to private schools. Eckes and Rapp (2006) have found that the variability in charter schools complicates efforts to compare them as a category to public schools, and Metcalf and Paul (2006) report only very modest achievement differences in students with vouchers who attend private school versus public school.

Within the exosystem, the various organizations in a student's community have exerted influence on the critical issue of school reform; as a result, multiple models have emerged, each with varying effects. These models, however, do not examine all aspects of a student's experience in the preparation for college. Policymakers operating at the exosystem level typically examine only those factors existing within the school environment that are part of a reform effort. A larger, more complete view using the ecological framework would also examine the student's experience from other levels of the model.

Role of States

State and federal initiatives designed to affect students' college readiness also exist at the exosystem level. These initiatives exert their influence through policy development, school reform across whole districts or states, and the creation of common standards. The research that examines reform efforts on the state level attempts to identify patterns of success in policies or programs that support college preparation and access.

Many states' school reform efforts focus on alignment of the curriculum through standards and policies and the measurement of achievement through common assessments. As states work toward increasing alignment between their school and college systems, they implement a range of policies, including the establishment of graduation requirements, specification of college admissions standards, and new criteria for the distribution of financial aid.

In *Claiming Common Ground*, the National Center for Public Policy and Higher Education examines K–16 alignment from a state policy perspective (Callan and others, 2006). The authors identify four policy levers that states can use to improve college readiness, and that characterize many of the current efforts:

- Statewide data systems that provide the ability to track individual students' progress and course taking throughout their educational careers and into the workforce.
- Alignment of course work and assessments so that curricula and tests in K–12 schools and in the first years of college are complementary with and connected to each other.
- State finance and budgeting tools (such as cross-sector funding, funding for dual enrollment, and financial incentives for accountability) to improve P–16 collaboration.
- Accountability efforts to hold institutions accountable for student progress and success from preschool through college.

Another organization, JFF, made its recommendations for state policy on school reform in a report targeted to state governors (Kazis, Pennington, and Conklin, 2003). In this report, JFF analyzes the "leaky education pipeline" and makes recommendations that support better alignment in K–16 that are similar to the *Claiming Common Ground* report.

To varying degrees, each state has developed initiatives to increase the college attendance of its students. In most cases, the state itself publishes research on the success of its efforts. Throughout the literature, the review of these programs typically results in a state or federally commissioned report, often supported by funding from a foundation or other private organization, describing the efforts and results: what has worked, what has been less effective, and the barriers to success. Efforts range from allowing high school juniors and seniors to take college courses with state funds following them (Pennington, 2004) to the alignment of high school standards with state university entrance requirements (Tafel and Eberhart, 1999; Tierney and Garcia, 2008). The themes of accountability and alignment are prevalent in statewide reforms and are in part directed by legislation and policy work at the federal level.

Role of Federal Government

The federal government, in collaboration with state governments, has played a significant role in school reform by emphasizing academic achievement and the development of K–12 standards and by influencing financial aid policy for higher education. These exosystem-level activities have profound indirect effects on students' abilities to achieve college readiness and access.

Since its passage in 2001, the federal education legislation No Child Left Behind (NCLB) has exerted a strong influence on state educational policy. To comply with NCLB, states must engage in standardized outcomes testing, and schools must be held accountable if student test scores do not show improvement over time. One wide-reaching influence resulting from NCLB is the Comprehensive School Reform (CSR) effort sponsored by states and the U.S. Department of Education, providing funds for school systems implementing reform models. CSR emphasizes systemic change within a school and focuses particularly on curricular reform and assessment. Much of the available funding has been tied to Title I, targeting schools with high percentages of low-income students (St. John, 2006), and most reform models emphasize changes to the high school curriculum. For example, AVID and America's Choice programs were developed to prepare underachieving students for a four-year college education by restructuring the high school curriculum and pedagogy (Haskins and Kemple, 2009; Martinez and Klopott, 2005).

Other reform models, such as the Coalition of Essential Schools and First Things First are designed to create strong relationships between and among students and adults and improve the social dimensions of schools by creating smaller learning communities (Martinez and Klopott, 2005; Quint, 2001). The federal government's funding of these reform models has had a strong influence on the student's immediate learning environment, although the policy planning and reform model designs happen at the exosystem level.

Standards

Along with various efforts supporting school reform, the federal government's educational policy has focused on alignment through the development of common K–12 curriculum standards (Martinez and Klopott, 2005). The standards movement attempts to provide a legislated means for establishing common expectations for all students and an enforceable policy for creating equitable education across diverse schools and student populations. Although these common standards are developed at the exosystem level, the hope of policymakers is to create a smoother transition to college readiness for students on an individual level.

The origins of the current standard movement began when private organizations such as Achieve, the Fordham Foundation, and the National Alliance of Business and Education Trust launched the National Diploma Project as a way of developing standards at the K–12 and college juncture. The data to support this effort were supplied in large part by analyses derived from Achieve's work with large-scale tests. The Benchmarks document that summarizes this work led to the development of National Core Standards articulating a set of "college and career-ready" standards supported by the National Board of Governors and Council of Chief State School Officers (Haycock, 2006). Although implementation details of the standards movement vary depending on the political climate, the federal government's continued funding of standards implementation focuses attention on the movement. The setting of standards and the development of alignment policies occur in the exosystem outside students' immediate environment; however, students encounter the effects of standards implementation in the courses and tests that serve as gatekeepers to the next level of educational achievement.

Financing Higher Education

The policies regarding the distribution of grant aid at the state, federal, and institutional levels also exist at the exosystem level. These policies have a profound effect on a student's ability to afford a higher education degree, particularly among students from low-income backgrounds.

Historically, the principal vehicle for providing college access to low-income students has been the Pell Grant. Created in 1972 as the Basic Education Opportunity Grant, the Pell Grant program has enabled millions of students from low-income families to attend two- and four-year colleges. The investments in this program, however, have not kept pace with either college costs or the rising demand for college. Over time, the Pell Grant has covered less and less of the cost of college attendance, reducing access for thousands of students from low-income families. In contrast, federal expenditures on non-need-based student aid have grown exponentially faster over the past decade than expenditures on need-based aid (St. John, 2006).

States are a smaller player in student aid but a significant one nonetheless. Although state expenditures on need-based aid have increased substantially over time, state expenditures on non-need-based grants have increased more dramatically. Like their federal counterparts, state lawmakers have voted for the biggest increases in student aid for middle- and upper-income families rather than lower-income families (St. John, 2004). These policies and practices affect the students and communities of low-income students and shape their experience as they attempt to become college ready.

On the higher education level, most colleges have traditionally deployed their own monetary resources to meet the demonstrated financial needs of the low-income students they admit. However, beginning in the late 1970s and increasing since then, schools began to use a set of practices known as enrollment management to change the way financial aid was distributed (Hossler, Schmit, and Vesper, 1999). Enrollment management was not primarily directed at access to college through financial aid. Instead, institutions used enrollment management strategies for two very different purposes: first, to "purchase" the high school talent that would boost their prestige in ranking guides; and second, to shield middle- and upper-class students and their families who were reluctant to pay full price from the rapidly escalating cost of attending the nation's colleges and universities. Haycock (2006) argues that this shift in enrollment management has significantly and negatively affected the access of low-income students to college, particularly to private colleges.

In their work, Deming and Dynarski (2009) review experimental and quasi-experimental research on the relationship between college costs and educational attainment, with a particular focus on low-income populations. Evidence indicates that reducing college costs can increase college entry and persistence. Programs that are simple and transparent and link money to incentives or academic support services, or both, appear to be particularly effective for this population. At the exosystem level of the ecological model, changes to financial aid policy that introduce barriers to the process of receiving financial aid or increased college costs have a significant and negative effect on the experience of individual students as they navigate toward college.

Role of Foundations and Nonprofit Organizations

Although many of the programs we have cited in this chapter have state and federal government sponsorship, the role of private organizations and foundations has increased dramatically. Many of these organizations have partnered with government agencies and other nonprofits. Foundations have been significant players in the evaluation of programs and the development of successful programs. Like the federal and state governments, foundations exert an enormous influence at the exosystem level, shepherding resources toward policies and practices that have powerful effects on individual students. Here we look at a few key players in the area of college readiness and access.

The Bill and Melinda Gates Foundation has funded multiple endeavors, including the Common Core Standards and Early College High Schools efforts described earlier. One of its most significant intervention efforts began in 2001, when the Gates Foundation launched the ten-year multimillion-dollar Washington State Achievers Program to increase opportunities for low-income students to attend postsecondary institutions in Washington (Ramsey and Gorgol, 2010). Similarly, the Gates Millennium Scholars program sponsors college attendance, removing financial barriers for talented low-income students (Deming and Dynarski, 2009). The Gates Foundation has systemically searched for ways to have a long-lasting influence on school systems and nationwide reform efforts with a focus on college readiness and completion.

The Pathways to College Network, supported by Institute for Higher Education Policy, is an alliance of thirty-eight national organizations and funders committed to advancing college access and success for underserved students, including those who are the first in their families to go to college, low-income students, underrepresented minorities, and students with disabilities (Pathways to College Network, 2002). Similarly, the Lumina Foundation has played an important role in identifying significant barriers on the path to college and is known for its excellent evaluations of programs (Lumina Foundation,

2008). Foundations operating at this exosystem level emphasize the connection of policymakers, education leaders, practitioners, and community leaders with research on effective strategies for improving college preparation and enrollment.

Higher education institutions also have played a critical role in the funding and support of these programs. As an example, the long-standing Talent Development High Schools (TDHS) model was developed by the Johns Hopkins Center for Research on the Education of Students Placed at Risk. The program was designed to help schools prepare all students to succeed in a high-standards curriculum and in their careers. TDHS primarily targets schools that face serious problems with student attendance, discipline, achievement scores, and dropout rates, promoting smaller learning communities (Martinez and Klopott, 2005).

Unlike the state and federal governments, foundations and private organizations can look beyond the political environments of the current day across systems and take greater risks in their investment in various programs. Beyond providing critical financial support, they also offer evaluation-based insights on the most effective ways to achieve student outcomes. There is an increasing pattern of collaboration among foundations and the state and federal government, leading to more comprehensive cross-systems and cross-level reforms. When these large policy influences converge in the exosystem, individual students experience their effects through the programs and reforms that emerge.

Systems and Structures in Ecological Context

The exosystem encompasses the various influences of the organizations and policies surrounding individual students and their subsequent effects on college readiness and access. These influences include school- and nonschool-based college readiness program design; curriculum reform and assessment at the school, district, and state levels; private organization and foundation initiatives; and government policies that affect students' ability to be admitted to college and obtain financial aid.

In the body of literature analyzing these exosystem-level factors, however, there is relatively little information about what works for individual students, with their own complicated set of developmentally instigative characteristics, circumstances, and backgrounds. At the exosystem level, focal outcomes are demonstrated by aggregate data: high school graduation rates, college acceptance statistics, and postsecondary persistence rates. There are few examples of exosystem entities that have been coordinated even at a high level—across intervention program design, school reform, and government policy, for example. Although it is at the micro- and mesosystem levels that students experience reform efforts, these programs typically operate in isolation or with only one connection, rarely linking together all of the necessary elements needed for success of an individual student.

Tierney and Venegas (2009) studied broad financial aid programs in several contexts and found that thousands of students eligible for financial aid did not apply for support. They uncovered a separation between state policies and students' understanding of the steps they needed to accomplish in order to access financial aid. Tierney and Venegas emphasize that the students' cultural framework or the contexts in which they live have a direct impact on how they receive information regarding policies designed to remove barriers to college access. In the ecological model, the student experiences the environment through the level of the microsystem; if the policies implemented at the exosystem level do not correspond effectively with the cultural context of the microsystem, they will be ineffective in helping the students they were designed to support.

Some researchers have identified the importance of multiple support systems—such as the combination of academic support and easy access to financial aid (Haskins and Kemple, 2009)—as critical factors influencing the development of program design and reform initiatives at the level of policy and organizational structure. Similarly, some programs, such as the Washington Achievers, are comprehensive and attempt to address students' needs at multiple levels of their ecological system. It is at the intersection of the many levels in a student's experience that truly comprehensive and effective approaches can be achieved that not only address broad policy issues and systemic changes but also take into account the cultural contexts of the students they serve.

Macrosystem: The Arena of Culture and Ideology

THE MACROSYSTEM IS THE BROADEST level of the environment, consisting of the culture and ideology that shape social structures, opportunities, and individual expectations. The structure of U.S. federalism and the constitutional powers of the federal government account for the state locus of K–12 schooling and the absence of a nationalized system of postsecondary education. Broad changes in demography and higher education occur because of macrosystem changes such as scientific and technological progress, postindustrialization, and globalization. These larger environmental factors account for the need for mass higher education, the characteristics of the student population, and the nature of differential advantage in American society. The problem of social inequality in college readiness arises because of such macrolevel forces, which press the need for postsecondary education while presenting structural obstacles to its accomplishment.

Foundational Beliefs

Ideologies of individualism, meritocracy, rationalism, and market capitalism underlie institutional arrangements and public discourses about higher education. Americans have long held to an overarching cultural belief in the ability of individuals to forge their own life paths and improve their circumstances through personal initiative. This meritocratic argument assumes that a combination of individual ability and hard work is rewarded through educational accomplishment, including admission to postsecondary institutions (Gelber, 2007; Hearn, 1984; McNamee and Miller, 2009).

The ideology of social mobility through personal initiative also assumes that institutions and individuals operate effectively in a market economy in which students and families make rational decisions about various opportunities to capitalize most effectively on their investments of time and money. Formal education is seen as the primary mechanism through which the meritocracy operates, with increasing emphasis on higher education as a private good that benefits individual investment in the postgraduate labor market. Although a minority of Americans believe college should not be for everyone (Symonds, Schwartz, and Ferguson, 2011), the prevailing macrosystem view is one of college for all (Rosenbaum, 2011). In one national survey, parents, teachers, and business executives agreed that college and career readiness were highly important. The three stakeholder groups differed, however, in what they thought college and career readiness meant, how high a priority each should be, and what schools and colleges should do to support readiness (MetLife, 2011).

In addition to assuming direct connections among opportunities, behaviors, and outcomes, economic ideologies also shape educational reform approaches such as standards and accountability (Aldeman, 2010; Kazis, Pennington, and Conklin, 2003). Market ideology supports privatization of higher education, in which institutions and individuals, rather than states or the federal government, are responsible for providing their own resources (Priest, St. John, and Boon, 2006). Within the framework of a societal market system, public colleges and universities participate directly in the marketplace.

Commercialization is one response of higher education, in which educational institutions "compete with private enterprises in the larger economic marketplace" (Priest, St. John, and Boon, 2006, p. 2). Marketization is another response, in which universities focus on economically lucrative activities such as graduate education, applied research, and entrepreneurial efforts (Mars, Slaughter, and Rhoades, 2008; Slaughter and Leslie, 1999; Slaughter and Rhoades, 2004). Prescribed secondary school curricula, high-stakes testing, and high loan burdens all flow from these macrosystem factors to affect students' college readiness and postsecondary pathways.

The macrosystem also contains the forces underlying the U.S. social structure. Meritocracy and market beliefs legitimize wide disparities in wealth across social groups. Ideologies of equal opportunity exist alongside institutionalized racism, as critical race theorists have pointed out. American beliefs about race and ethnicity support residential ethnic segregation. Neighborhood racial, ethnic, and income stratification is tied to school segregation and systematic disparities in family, community, and school resources (Reardon, 2011). Unequal distribution of opportunities for Advanced Placement courses among high schools, for instance, tracks closely with neighborhood socioeconomic status (Hallett and Venegas, 2011). Broad societal views of national sovereignty and identity affect the experiences and opportunities of documented and undocumented immigrants (Portes, 1999).

Language, Subculture, and Theory

The macrosystem level is enshrined in language that masks ideology and culture. For instance, Iverson (2012) demonstrated how concepts of deficit and marginality are built into the central terms of higher education policy discourse. In another analysis of higher education language, Pasque (2007) uncovered conflicting macrolevel ideologies in the discourse of different higher education leaders and speculated about the ways in which such unarticulated assumptions might drive policy. Conversations about the purpose of higher education, she writes, were founded on "competing visions, paradigms, and worldviews. These leaders (legislators, university presidents, national association leaders, faculty, and administrators) often talk about higher education's responsibility to serve society in extremely different ways and may—intentionally or unintentionally—labor against each other" (p. 40).

St. John (2007) and others have documented changes in the macrosystem view of college access by tracing changes in the policy conversation across the past thirty years. According to this analysis, the macrosystem view of education is reflected in a shift in language from an emphasis on equity and affirmative action to a focus on excellence and accountability. Along with higher education privatization and marketization, political attention to the middle class has shifted discourse, policy, and opportunity in the arena of college readiness. These shifts, in turn, can be understood as ideological responses to changing economies and labor markets that have occurred in response to globalization. Taken together, these broad currents in the macrosystem have resulted in a "devaluing of equity issues within the mainstream discourse of educational policy" (St. John, 2007, p. 387). To the extent that opportunity enters the discourse at all, the cultural view has shifted from an emphasis on race to one of socioeconomic status (Karabel, 2005; Tienda and others, 2003).

These ideologies of the dominant culture infuse the arena of college readiness for all U.S. students and educational institutions. The ecology of many educationally and economically challenged students additionally contains macrosystem elements of nondominant cultures. Values of remaining in close proximity to family, for instance, are characteristic of collectivist Latino and rural populations (Beasley, 2011; Stanton-Salazar 2011). Most research and policy on college readiness assumes a dominant culture macrosystem. The cultural integrity model, in contrast, focuses on incongruence between the dominant culture and subcultural beliefs and practices as an obstacle to readiness among students whose school and home cultures differ (Tierney and Jun, 2001).

Theory itself is a carrier of ideology, as Tierney and Venegas (2009) stress. Status attainment theory, human capital theory, and rational choice theory are leading approaches to scholarship and policymaking in college readiness (Tierney and Venegas, 2009; Walpole, 2007). These theories conform to cultural beliefs in opportunity, merit-based advancement, and rational decision making that place responsibility for college readiness squarely on the individual. Critical theories and social reproduction theories, in contrast, portray social inequalities as the result of structural arrangements that legitimize unequal power relations in the greater society (Bourdieu, 1977; Bourdieu and Passeron, 1977; Tornatzky, Cutler, and Lee, 2002; Walpole, 2007; Winkle-Wagner, 2010). Differences in academic disciplines also frame macroassumptions about college readiness, as when psychologists focus on individual traits or economists on labor force opportunities (Perna, 2007; Perna and Thomas, 2008; Walpole, 2007).

Critical scholars who address the macrosystem level of the environment generally point out the shortcomings in economic models of rational choice that presume equal access to high-quality precollege schooling and complete information about higher education (Tierney and Venegas, 2009; Walpole,

2007; Winkle-Wagner, 2010). Researchers also deconstruct the language of higher education policy to show its hidden values assumptions (Iverson, 2012; Pasque, 2007; St. John, 2007). Social reproduction scholars and other critical theorists draw attention to the ways in which culturally specific normative practices are disguised as neutral and universal so that their differential effects are attributed to shortcomings in individuals rather than structures (McDonough, 1997; Walpole, 2007; Winkle-Wagner, 2010). The dominant policy discourse, however, remains embedded in an economic ideology of individual attainment through a fair system of standardized educational opportunity, individual rational choice, quantitative measurement of student outcomes, and institutional accountability.

Because the macrosystem contains the fundamental ideas of the society, it influences all of the other levels of the environment. It also responds to other levels of the environment. For instance, collective political pressure and the self-interest of higher education institutions have converged over the past forty years to expand access to higher education for African Americans, according to Karabel (2005). Karabel sees no parallel political movement and institutional advantage driving expanded access to college success for low-income groups.

Culture and Ideology in the Ecological Context

In a *Chronicle of Higher Education* commentary, Hilary Pennington of the Bill and Melinda Gates Foundation argues that "institutions should improve student success by focusing on practices within their control instead of blaming external factors" (2012, para. 4). While Pennington is correct that institutional practices affect student success, an ecological view that includes external factors is essential to understanding and changing persistent educational disparities among demographic groups. An ecological model draws attention to the ways in which macrosystem elements are embedded in policy decisions and educational practices. Bringing ideological assumptions to the surface is necessary for policy debates, as well as culturally relevant educational practice.

The connections between educational outcomes and social structures need to be articulated and debated in the larger society. Educational institutions do need to take responsibility within their purview. Without an external view, however, educators and policymakers risk blaming individual students for social ills, overlooking strengths within underrepresented groups, and perpetuating practices based on faulty assumptions. The successive equality movements of the past sixty years demonstrate the connections among awareness, activism, and social change. Most fundamental, attention to the macrosystem enables grassroots microsystem pressure and policy-level exosystem efforts to modify social beliefs and drive institutional change.

Chronosystem: The Role of Time in College Readiness

THE MACROSYSTEM CHANGES in response to pressure from other levels of the environment, including the final component of the human ecology model: the chronosystem. These changes are a result of the movements, events, and shifting ideologies associated with historical time. The chronosystem also includes other temporal elements of environmental change, such as sequential processes, chronological age, generational cohort, and developmental growth. The intersection of an individual life, timing, and sociohistorical context are key determinants of educational outcomes. Bronfenbrenner's (1979, 1993; Bronfenbrenner and Morris, 2006) model of person-process-context-time enables analysis of the dynamic effects of time on college readiness.

Cohort and Era

The most obvious connection between the macrosystem and chronosystem is in the experience of same-age cohorts who encounter a historical context together. For example, contemporary students are coming of age in an era in which college aspirations are responsive to the rise of mass higher education and the disappearance of U.S. manufacturing jobs in a globalized labor market (Kim and Rury, 2007). Successive equality movements continue to reshape cultural beliefs about roles and opportunities for women; people of color; people with disabilities; and gay, lesbian, bisexual, and transgender individuals (Karabel, 2005). The broad macrosystem ideological shift from race-based to socioeconomic-based affirmative admissions affects the educational chances of students who are eligible for admission and scholarships such as the Georgia Hope scholarship or the Texas top 10 percent state university admission policy (St. John, 2007; Tienda and others, 2003).

Historical trends enter the exosystem level in time-bound political and legislative movements that reach students through arenas such as federal financial aid policy (Gullat and Jan, 2003). Current students experience an education era shaped by No Child Left Behind legislation and the broader standards and accountability movements (Barnes and Slate, 2010). More tightly time-bound events such as the recession of 2008 affect a particular cohort through decreased family resources, scarce summer jobs, and the tightening of credit for private loans. Political realities, including state budgets for public higher education and federal financial aid availability, vary across time and are experienced differentially according to students' age. Intergenerational effects are other time factors affecting how students experience and engage their immediate environments. Student socioeconomic status, of course, is a factor of family history, including the influential role of parental education on student college behaviors (Bailey and Dynarski, 2011; Currie and Moretti, 2002; Reardon, 2011). Personal and family immigration history and timing play roles in attitudes and knowledge about higher education (Tornatzky, Cutler, and Lee, 2002). In all of these cases, changes in the macrosystem and exosystem occur through historically bound events and social movements that intersect with the timing of students' individual and linked biographies (Bonous-Hammarth and Allen, 2005; Elder and Shanahan, 2006).

Sequence and Timing

Education occurs over time. Metaphors of pipelines or pathways are central, time-based conceptions of college readiness as consisting of sequential events, tasks, or stages. The prominent Lumina Foundation (2009) integrates its efforts under the umbrella terms of college "pathways" and "continuum" and calls for a "pipeline of services." Recommendations for connecting levels of education to support smooth transitions between middle school and high school and between high school and college rest on this idea of education as a continuous path (Hodgkinson, 1999; Venezia and Kirst, 2005). Hossler and

Gallagher's (1987) influential theory of college choice, which includes the stages of predisposition, search, and choice, assumes a temporally ordered educational sequence, as do more elaborated versions of steps toward higher education (Cabrera and La Nasa, 2000; Hossler, Braxton, and Coopersmith, 1989).

College readiness research bears out a sequential conception in some instances but not others. For instance, it is clearly important for high school students to take courses that enable them to meet admission standards for colleges and to attain sufficient academic skills for success in higher education (Cabrera and La Nasa, 2000; Lumina Foundation, 2009). There is widespread consensus that high school academic preparation is at the heart of college readiness (Adelman, 1999; Bedsworth, Colby, and Doctor, 2006). Although there is no corresponding agreement on how best to provide that preparation, stakeholders generally point to the importance of taking gateway courses such as Algebra 2 before entering college (Checkley, 2001). Graduating from high school, taking a college entrance examination, completing applications, and filling out financial aid forms are steps that typically occur before entering postsecondary education (Cabrera and La Nasa, 2000). When high school students complete college-preparatory courses, testing, and applications, they are more likely to enter college (Mazzeo, 2010). When they attend college directly after high school, they are more likely to persist and earn a degree (Goldrick-Rab, Carter, and Wagner, 2007; Goldrick-Rab and Han, 2011). These patterns involve sequences in which educational outcomes are associated with particular sequences of actions that take place in settings tied to chronological age.

The timing of college preparation tasks and educational interventions is an important chronosystem issue that has received little research attention (Hoxby, 2004; Perna and Swail, 2001). College entrance testing and application and notification deadlines follow a national calendar in which certain steps must be completed at particular times to move directly from high school to most colleges. The importance of adherence to multiple deadlines is apparent, for instance, in the U.S. Department of Education's "College Preparation Checklist," which provides a listing of student and parent time-lined tasks (U.S. Department of Education, 2003). Research in the Chicago school district shows that filling out the Free Application for Federal Student Aid financial aid documents in the senior year of high school is a key indicator of a graduate's college enrollment in the following year (Mazzeo, 2010). Even college-intending students are adversely affected by failing to complete college preparation tasks on time. Policy scholars have drawn attention to the timing of testing as a factor in college enrollments among economically and educationally challenged youth. Even if high school tests are well aligned with college skills, students need sufficiently early feedback and time to make up any deficiencies in their college readiness after taking tests (Hayward, Brandes, Kirst, and Mazzeo, 1997; Tierney and Garcia, 2008).

Many economically and educationally challenged students do not follow an orderly sequence from middle school through high school in which they first decide to pursue a college degree, prepare appropriately, and then complete serial college search, application, and choice tasks (Arnold and others, 2009). Students outside typical educational tracks include those who have disengaged or dropped out of high school (Steinberg and Allen, 2011), GED holders (Zhang, 2010), and adults (Zafft, Kallenbach, and Spohn, 2006). Even students who graduate from high school at age eighteen after continuous enrollment do not necessarily travel a sequential path to college. For example, for low-income families, perceptions of college costs and financial aid availability shape college aspirations before high school and interact over time with all other higher education decisions (Tierney and Venegas, 2007). Students in dual-enrollment and early college high schools enter higher education before college choice and selection take place (Pennington, 2004). A growing body of research shows that even college-intending students who have been accepted to college and applied for financial aid continue to consider whether and where to attend college during the summer following high school graduation (Arnold and others, 2009; Castleman, Arnold, and Wartman, 2012).

An educational pathway or pipeline is characterized by transitions that can also be classified as chronosystem factors. Students are particularly vulnerable to obstacles associated with transitions from one level of the educational system to the next. The move from middle school to high school, for instance, is a critical junction during which students make decisions about courses that will affect their college eligibility (Friedman, 2006; Gibbons and Borders, 2010; Hoffman and Vargas, 2010).

The transition from high school to college is the key passage in which educationally and economically challenged students encounter a variety of obstacles that result in less frequent, delayed, and lower-quality college enrollments. Most policy, research, and intervention programs in the arena of college readiness address the transition from high school to college. Viewing the move between high school and college as a chronosystem factor focuses attention on the longitudinal nature of educational progress and the structural discontinuities in the overall education system (Hodgkinson, 1999; Venezia and Kirst, 2005). Policy efforts to align K–16 academic skills and content knowledge attempt to smooth transitions across levels of the educational systems. Some intervention and outreach programs work across feeder systems of schools, for instance, by placing academically talented low-income students into highly selective high schools or working within a linked set of elementary and middle schools that sends students into particular high schools (Snipes, Holton, Doolittle, and Sztejnberg, 2006).

The timing and duration of interventions also fall into the chronosystem. Perna and Swail (2001) note that despite calls for early intervention, "more research is required to determine the most appropriate level at which students should initially become involved in an early intervention program" (p. 105). They go on to note that the College Board's national survey of college outreach programs found that intervention programs commonly begin in the ninth grade, as students enter high school (Swail, 2000; Perna and Swail, 2001). The initial formation of college aspirations and decisions about college preparatory tracks take place before high school, however, so many researchers call for intervention to begin in the middle school years (Cabrera and others, 2006; Kennelly and Monrad, 2007; Wimberly and Noeth, 2005). The federally funded GEAR UP program begins in middle school, as does the well-studied Indiana 21st Century Scholars Program (Lumina Foundation, 2008).

Program duration over time relates to higher education outcomes. In a study of college readiness programs, Gandara and Bial (2001) found that the most successful programs occurred over long periods and multiple years. Gandara (2002, 2004) replicated this finding in her evaluations of the Puente project, while Hayward, Brandes, Kirst, and Mazzeo (1997) noted similar positive effects of sustained duration in partnerships among schools, programs, and higher education institutions. Other scholars have identified the importance of sustained school engagement (Kennelly and Monrad, 2007) and consistent parental involvement (Fann, McClafferty Jarsky, and McDonough, 2009), although their work is not as empirically founded. As Tierney (2004) states: "The academic problems that students face after years of substandard schooling most likely cannot be remedied in a short period . . . Because problems are longitudinal, programs should be designed to take place over time. They will be long-term rather than stopgap" (pp. 960–961).

Developmental Change

Environments and ideologies change with the passage of time and as students encounter experiences and tasks that reflect changing ideas and historical events. At the same time, individuals and families themselves change systematically with the passage of time. For high school students, "issues of timing correlate with a period during the life course when maturation and previous developmental stages coalesce and enable students to acquire new skills sets" (Bonous-Hammarth and Allen, 2005, p. 156). For instance, the relative inability of teenagers to prioritize long-term goals is a normative developmental feature of adolescence that can disadvantage students without a knowledgeable adult to reinforce college aspirations and help negotiate college entry (Arnold and others, 2009). Adolescents' conception of time and possibilities for the future are not fully mature, as demonstrated in a study in which researchers found that low-achieving high school juniors "believe that high school would last forever and that it was never too late to turn things around in preparing for college or for other postsecondary options" (Gandara, Gutierrez, and O'Hara, 2001, p. 90). Although it makes sense to tie interventions to student development phases and capabilities, the recent work of Savitz-Romer and Bouffard (2012) is the only systematic treatment of the developmental aspects of college readiness.

Individual and family changes occur as a joint result of development and accompanying environmental change. For instance, parents' involvement with their children's education diminishes over time, with low-income families becoming less involved in late high school (Crosnoe, 2001; Gullatt and Jan, 2003). Other researchers have found that the aspirations of economically and educationally challenged students diminish over time (Berzin, 2010) and that the key college skill of reading ability follows a downward trend between tenth grade and high school graduation among this population (Vitale and Schmeiser, 2006). These alarming findings point to the complexity of the interacting changes in environments and individuals that occur as a function of time.

The Role of Time in Ecological Context

The chronosystem lens indicates that researchers, policymakers, and practitioners should consider the development of college readiness as longitudinal but not strictly sequential. Unlike the Hossler and Gallagher (1987) view of college choice as a reasonably orderly sequence of predisposition, search, and selection, low-income students experience a much more fluid pathway to higher education (Arnold and others, 2009). Financial aid is not the final step in the college access of students but instead plays a role from the earlier stage of deciding whether college is desirable or possible (Tierney and Venegas, 2009). As Perna and Thomas (2008) note, indicators of student success are "shaped in part by the attainment of other indicators of success" (p. 34).

In short, human ecologies occur within personal, social, and historical time. The temporal aspects of the ecology of college readiness have strong implications for interventions that consider the effects of development, chronological age, and time sensitive college decisions and preparation tasks.

The Ecological View of College Readiness

A S THE PRECEDING CHAPTERS DESCRIBE, college readiness has been the focus of extensive research, theory, policy, and practice over the past three decades. Despite all of this attention to the issue, however, large numbers of students continue to graduate from high school without the academic and practical knowledge they need to succeed in higher education. A major reason that increasing college readiness has proven so intractable is the complexity of the interacting personal, organizational, and societal factors in play. As Deil-Amen and Turley summarize, "many individual, family, institutional and system-wide factors simultaneously affect a person's ability to prepare, apply, enroll, finance, and graduate from college" (2007, p. 2357). Calls for integrative models that address the complexity of college readiness, span K–16, and account for individual and group variability appear regularly in the literature (Cabrera and others, 2006; Hayward, Brandes, Kirst, and Mazzeo, 1997; Louie, 2007).

What is needed in the field of "transition to college," Deil-Amen and Turley write, is "an emphasis on how the wider societal system of stratification and opportunity interact with individuals, social groups, and educational institutions in a dynamic interplay that affects opportunities for quality educational advancement" (2007, p. 2357). The best available theories of college access and success have attempted to account for this complexity (Padilla, 2009b; Perna, 2006; Tierney and Venegas, 2007), but the field of college readiness is still in search of approaches that fully account for the change processes resulting in dynamic, multidirectional interactions between varied individuals and multiple environments.

FIGURE 3
Ecological Model of College Readiness

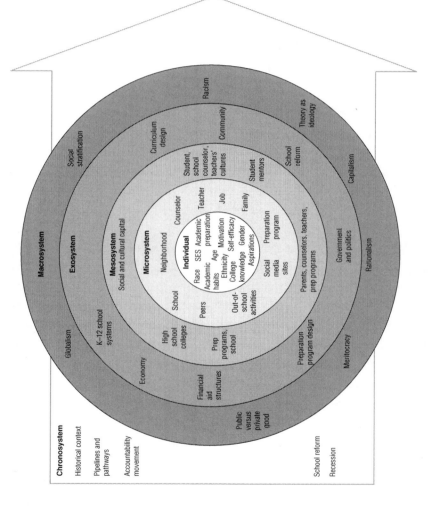

The leading environmental systems theory in the field of developmental psychology—Bronfenbrenner's theory of the ecology of human development—addresses the call for an integrative model and has much to offer the field of education. The person-process-context-time (PPCT) theory accounts for the complexity of college readiness by modeling the interplay of an active, developing person, and his or her nested environments. By centering on interactions, as opposed to isolating selected aspects of students and environments, the theory provides a way of understanding contextual influences on the educational trajectories of different demographic groups while also explaining how individual agency operates to differentiate outcomes within groups.

Figure 3 represents the major findings from the literature, mapped onto the corresponding levels of the environment. As depicted in Figure 3 and described previously, most researchers and policymakers have conceptualized college readiness according to distinct ecological levels such as student demography, educational and family settings, and organizational reforms. Even this level of analysis shows the advantages of Bronfenbrenner's conceptions of environmental levels in drawing attention to the underrepresentation of knowledge about mesosystem, macrosystem, and chronosystem influences.

Only the full ecological model, however, has the power to account for the interacting elements that together determine college readiness. According to the PPCT model, environments are more than additive: they are mutually constituting. Environments overlap and affect each other, as when a student's need to help support the family introduces him to an influential noncollege-bound peer group at an after-school workplace or a student's teacher pairs her with a college student tutor who influences her family's aspirations for their daughter.

Students develop the aspirations and behaviors that affect their academic preparation in light of opportunities, resources, hazards, and options that originate beyond their immediate environments. Economically and educationally challenged students shape their lives in response to forces such as financial aid availability, poor schools, residential segregation, racism, poverty, immigration policy, neighborhood violence, and devalued cultural capital. Large cultural currents of meritocracy, individualism, capitalism, and globalization mean that students form their postsecondary aspirations in light of the opportunity structure they face in a postindustrial, evolving labor market and perform the task of financing high college tuition within social systems that ask them to locate resources and take on sometimes crushing debt. In short, students encounter multiple interacting influences that emanate from both immediate and more distant levels of their social ecology. These environmental interactions, moreover, change over time and are profoundly affected by the characteristics of the individual encountering them.

The Ecology of College Readiness

College readiness is a challenging construct because it is multifaceted and holistic, varies by both individual and group characteristics, and combines elements that are within and outside students' control. The college-ready student possesses a set of content knowledge; academic strategies, skills, and dispositions; and psychosocial skills such as motivation and tolerance for complexity. College readiness also comprises higher education expectations and aspirations; knowledge about college and financial aid; and the skills and practical know-how to negotiate the complicated tasks of choosing, applying, selecting, and financing college.

The ecology of the individual student determines whether that student acquires the constellation of aspirations, dispositions, and academic and practical knowledge that constitute college readiness. Although shaped in each student's complete ecology, college readiness is a property of the individual. In an ecological perspective, academic preparation and other readiness attributes result from developmentally instigative characteristics that predispose the individual to acquire the skills and knowledge that will enable him or her to aspire to, enter, and succeed in college. This conception grants agency to individuals and explains individual differences. It starts from the assumption of student strengths rather than deficits. Importantly, individual-level traits that affect students' experiences and their responses to experiences are themselves formed through interactions with environmental conditions. A student who believes she cannot succeed academically and therefore avoids challenging herself in school, for instance, might have internalized this directive belief from her experiences, others' expectations of her, or media representations of her cultural group.

Key questions arise from the ecological view in which personal traits are seen as affecting how individuals experience environments and how they act to shape those environments. How do students employ instigative characteristics in college readiness tasks? What kinds of traits optimize college readiness, and what environmental conditions facilitate the development of these traits for particular kinds of students? How do different students both experience and respond to environments? How do students actively select and shape their environments? What environmental characteristics permit, elicit, or inhibit student agency? Such questions suggest a new focus on the elements of person-environment covariation in studying students, delivering college readiness programs, and evaluating educational interventions.

Contextual influences emanate from multiple sources, but individuals can be influenced only by direct interaction with the people, activities, roles, and objects with which they are in immediate contact. For example, "curriculum" is not a microsystem, but it enters microsystems when students encounter subject material in classrooms, books, and projects. Attending to the ways in which policies and program designs actually reach students is a key ecological concern connecting policy and organizational levels of the environment to the lived experience of students. Microsystems connect to the individual through their capacity to elicit or constrain participation among different kinds of students. The nature of participation is also important: developmentally beneficial microsystems demand sustained, progressively more complex cognitions and behaviors. As with characteristic dispositions for engagement, individuals differ in the amount of complexity they are willing or able to engage. The timing and sequence of environmental challenges are therefore key elements of effective microsystems, as is the provision of sufficient buffers against debilitating stress (Wachs, 1992). Because of these individual and temporal influences, no single practice, program, or setting will be equally effective for all students.

Students change as a result of their engagement within their immediate settings, relationships, and activities. They have many such immediate environments, however, and the combined set of overlapping microsystems forms their world. A mesosystem view of college readiness fixes attention on how the components of a student's life fit together. Not all contexts are equivalent for students in time commitment, psychological investment, or perceived importance. If a given experience is not the focus of time and investment by a student, its effects will be overcome by other areas of involvement. If the combined microsystems add up to an overloaded or chaotic total environment or if microsystems are fragmented, unengaging, or contradictory, positive experiences in individual microsystems—classes, peer groups, or college preparation programs—will be compromised or negated. Microsystems that reinforce each other through congruent messages and common membership amplify the developmental effects of individual settings. When the mesosystem features incongruent environments, as in the case of different cultural expectations in schools and families, students are less likely to experience the sustained, comprehensive proximal processes that lead to college readiness.

A mesosystem approach concentrates on the interaction of messages, experiences, and relationships across the settings and roles that students inhabit. From a policy and practice perspective, this lens suggests strategies to optimize cultural consonance, reinforce connections across environments, and encourage direct involvement of significant people in multiple settings. Congruence across student contexts calls for the promotion of active family and community involvement in schools and college preparation programs. The mesosystem approach underlines the value of experiences in which high school students spend time on college campuses rather than learn about college only within high schools and college readiness programs. The research literature to date supports these propositions, suggesting the need for additional research, policy, and practice that concentrate on the student mesosystem.

College readiness comes down to the individual's experience in his or her overlapping immediate environments. Those experiences in turn are affected by the structural arrangements of social institutions that are designed and modified at a level of the environment where students are not present. The exosystem level is key to structural change because it sets the ground rules for the opportunities, experiences, and environments that students encounter and determines how organizations, programs, and educational interventions embody these possibilities. Despite these exosystem roles, the potential for systems-level change is constrained by the confluence of different policies and the complexity of actors, organizations, stakeholders, issues, and history.

Within the exosystem itself, interactions across these elements can have fragmented and even clashing effects.

The entire college readiness issue is predicated on the need for a significant life course transition arising from the structural separation and temporal sequencing of K–12 and higher education. Students are indirectly but deeply affected by the general educational reform movement and associated practices of accountability and testing, curriculum reform, common standards, and data sharing. They also experience the effects of specific educational reforms emanating from the exosystem, such as innovative small schools, career academies, and early college high schools. The degree to which students' cultural capital is valued in formal education settings is another exosystem factor affecting their ability to negotiate the transition into higher education and the ways in which they are received there. Finally, the exosystem is the generator of structures of economic and racial inequality that contribute to disorganization and dysfunction within many low-income family, neighborhood, and school settings. A full ecological model focuses on the ways in which exosystem initiatives both derive from and influence social and cultural values in the macrosystem. The ways that educational policies, government actions, resource distribution, and organizational practices filter down to students' immediate experience is a central analytical category of an ecological approach to college readiness. Differential effects of programs and policies in varied contexts, and with different kinds of students, are also important areas for research and educational intervention.

At the broadest level of the ecology, macrosystems contain beliefs and ideologies that frame both the overall structure of schooling and the patterns of opportunities and perceived possibilities for different people. The macrosystem influences the ways dominant cultural and subcultural ideas and practices affect everything from policy (for example, rational choice models) to higher education costs (for example, individual responsibility for financing the private good of higher education) to individual aspirations (for example, perceptions of possible selves). Macrosystem factors show up in students' microsystems as cultural practices and contradictions and in experiences that teacher or counselor beliefs shape. They also find expression in exosystem policy and program design (Iverson, 2012; Pasque, 2007). Although the macrosystem cannot be manipulated directly, it is nonetheless worthwhile to articulate and debate macrosystem beliefs that drive policy or serve to reproduce social inequality.

Using an Ecological Approach in Research and Evaluation

Wachs (1992) provides a useful overview of how developmental systems models can be used in research and evaluation. He distinguishes three phases of contextually grounded developmental research. Phase I studies investigate the results of environment by comparing different groups. Much college readiness research is of this sort: the field has clearly identified the racial and socioeconomic categories that differentiate educational outcomes in the United States. This level of research does not deal with variability within groups, preexisting differences among groups, or context-specific effects of environments, however. Nor does it uncover the environmental factors that give rise to these group differences.

Phase II studies take up the question of which environmental variables are related to differences in development. Research of this type has demonstrated the kinds of environments and individual characteristics that make a difference in college readiness. The overriding importance of academic preparation in college access and success, for instance, is a phase II research finding, as is the emerging literature on the cognitive and psychosocial components of academic preparation. Most current methods of evaluation focus on particular aspects of a student's experience or the aggregate effects of a program or policy on large groups of students. Such studies can help guide policymakers and educators in determining the salient environmental parameters for intervention.

Knowing about and providing a particular developmentally advantageous experience is insufficient to ensure college readiness, however, because students are embedded in multiple contexts, they vary in their experience within any given context, and larger social forces act to shape these contexts. "To the extent that the environment functions as a system," Wachs notes, "the assumption that the whole equals the sum of its parts . . . may not be correct"

(1992, p. 150). Louie (2007) describes the evolution from phase I to phase II research and notes the limitations of the current state of knowledge:

> *The existing research has clearly shown that ascriptive individual-level characteristics such as race and socioeconomic status combined with institutional factors, including the quality and social climate of K–12 and postsecondary schooling, are the answer. It is how that occurs, specifically, how the individual negotiates and is received by the educational system, to become prepared for, get access to, obtain financing for, and complete college, that remains unanswered. In short, we need a more complex framework to understand how inequalities in these processes have been and continue to be created [p. 2223].*

Phase III research responds to Louie's call for a complex framework that accounts for processes that create individual variability within interconnected environments. According to Wachs (1992), this phase of investigation and intervention begins with the assumption of the existence of an environmental system and asks how environmental factors influence variability in development. In particular, phase III research investigates how higher-order environmental factors, such as family support or curriculum policy, influence development for different individuals. It also focuses on the process by which variability in environments relates to variability in development. For researchers, phase III ecological studies employ statistical techniques and qualitative methods that focus on multiple levels of ecological systems and on higher-order interactions. Wachs recommends that ecological researchers collect measures of the macrosystem (for example, specific cultural groups), individual characteristics (for example, different developmentally instigative characteristics), exosystem covariates (for example, instructional strategies that vary in effectiveness among different kinds of students), and contexts (for example, participation in certain programs, activities, or groups). Qualitative study methods are particularly well suited to studying individuals in context and proximal processes in environments (Bergerson, 2009; Goldrick-Rab and Han, 2011; Tierney and Venegas, 2009).

An ecological approach requires researchers to move beyond phase I and II studies of static demographic categories and isolated variables to investigate the formation, expression, and outcomes of developmentally instigative characteristics. Of specific interest are the contextual factors that interact with developmental change in students. Research is needed on how students choose relationships, activities, and settings and the ways in which they respond to those environments. The role of timing, life course patterns, and historical events is particularly underdeveloped in the college readiness literature. Ecological research requires major attention to what is actually occurring in students' microsystems and what conditions affect their responses and engagement in proximal processes of increasing complexity. To achieve this end, more rigorous evaluation of specific educational practices, programs, and interventions is needed. Scholars have repeatedly called for evaluations that use strong sampling procedures, control groups, longitudinal designs, cost-benefit analyses, and sophisticated statistical techniques (Gullat and Jan, 2003; Hayward, Brandes, Kirst, and Mazzeo, 1997; Long, 2007; Perna and Swail, 2001; Schultz and Mueller, 2006).

Because researchers and evaluators have rarely framed college readiness ecologically, only a small set of studies single out the ways in which different educational and personal contexts affect each other. Statistical models that isolate the predictive power of single variables or factors, in fact, ignore information about how microsystems interact. For instance, a researcher used logistic regression analysis to conclude that "friends' plans are found to be the single best predictor of 4-year college enrollment for low-income urban minority students, *even when controlling for* variables traditionally assumed to affect college going" (Sokatch, 2006, p. 128, italics added). This conventional analysis strategy disallowed mesosystem questions such as how friends are connected to other aspects of students' lives and how interacting circles of peers, family, community, and school settings collectively affect college readiness. These sorts of questions enable examination of which influences prevail in incongruent microsystem interactions, including, for example, whether academically ambitious friends trump uninvolved parents in student academic behaviors. The college readiness effects of connections across schools, programs, family, and friends are largely unstudied. Even less is known about the interconnections of educational experiences with student roles such as employee, sibling caregiver, or parent.

At the exosystem level, many college readiness policies and programs are intended to be wide reaching to affect as many students as possible. Policymakers seek a big-picture view of the effectiveness of reform efforts, requiring evaluations to assess the return on the considerable funding and structural support expended on implementation. Methodologies for evaluation range from in-depth quantitative studies using multiple variables to qualitative case studies. Few studies look across multiple programs, examine patterns in various efforts across different policy levels, address mesosystem interactions, or investigate effects of policy on individual students' microsystems. Even the most comprehensive studies of best practices in college-access reform initiatives (Martinez and Klopott, 2005) and college readiness programs (Schultz and Mueller, 2006; Swail, 2000) fail to address the range of environmental interactions highlighted by human ecology theory.

In their case study of seventeen college preparatory programs, Tierney and Hagedorn (2007) identify the key characteristics for model programs and make sweeping recommendations for improvements, including the creation of integrated structures with schools and colleges, coordinated funding structures, academic and counseling support, and tracking systems to monitor the progress of students. Their recommendations encompass multiple exosystem factors, along with individual, microsystem, and mesosystem elements, providing one of the most ecologically comprehensive approaches in the literature.

Despite these exemplary evaluations and program design recommendations, however, no model captures all ecological levels in the student's journey toward college readiness. Several, like Tierney and Hagedorn's, examine elements across the exosystem and microsystems that are necessary for successful student experiences but leave out critical influences from the overlapping individual and macrosystem levels.

Implications for Policy

Developmental systems models for college readiness policymakers, organizational leaders, and program designers have several large implications. As with scholars and evaluators, the many stakeholders in the exosystem need to understand that any attempt to improve college readiness involves an environmental system. This fundamental principle means that policy must account for the interactions of multiple environments and interventions that affect the operation of any given initiative. Providing additional financial aid to students will be ineffective if students do not believe they can afford college or do not understand how to access available funds, for instance. Increasing student aspirations or knowledge about applying to college will be futile if students are not academically prepared to succeed once they have enrolled (Deil-Amen and Turley, 2007). An ecological lens implies the need for programs, policies, and coordinating efforts that affect students across the settings of their lives, attend to cultural integrity, and knit together the elements of college readiness. A developmental systems approach also calls for attention to the ways in which the intersection of social structures and the macrofactors of culture and ideology function to support or disrupt the educational pathways of economically and educationally challenged students.

The second fundamental ecological principle for policy formulation is that change occurs within students as a result of interactions between person and environment in settings in which students are directly engaged. Classroom instruction, for instance, is where students experience the effects of curriculum and accountability: attempts at systemic change must include mechanisms to reach the classroom and other student settings with appropriate proximal processes. Policymakers can also use ecological perspectives to understand how different students are likely to encounter the effects of policies and program designs and how they might be induced to respond positively to structures, programs, opportunities, and information campaigns. Besides efforts to ensure that initiatives reach students in their daily lives and account for variability in individual responses and local contexts, policymakers need to attend to unanticipated, attenuated, and absent effects in students' microsystems. In a dramatic example, Mazzeo (2010) found that a new mandate requiring all Chicago Public School students to follow a rigorous college preparatory curriculum achieved the framers' goals of eliminating socioeconomic and racial gaps in course taking. Other outcomes, however, included a decline in grades, increased failure in mathematics courses, more absenteeism, and lower overall high school graduation and college enrollment rates. Interestingly, Mazzeo's response to this distressing situation was a call for improved instruction and student engagement, precisely the kinds of microsystem proximal processes implied by the ecological model.

Because no school or preparation program can offer the full range of environments and services required for college readiness, exosystem stakeholders can take action to connect and integrate interventions. Integration of efforts for comprehensive, sustained interventions will require collaboration across stakeholders in the exosystem (Hammick, Freeth, Copperman, and Goodsman, 2009; Lumina Foundation, 2009). Foundations are particularly well positioned to facilitate connections across government, K–12 schools, higher education, and community-based organizations and actors. Foundations such as Bill and Melinda Gates and Lumina are already taking leadership in articulating and coordinating exosystem initiatives across stakeholders. Finally, policymakers and organizational leaders need to articulate the macrosystem cultural beliefs that underlie their work, pushing against assumptions—such as student deficits or rational choice processes—that blame students for the effects of the larger ecology in which their lives unfold.

Implications for Practice

As in research and policy arenas, most schools and college readiness programs fail to address the multiple contexts and tasks involved in college access and success. Teachers, counselors, school leaders, and preparation program staff need to understand the ways in which students experience and make use of classrooms and program activities according to their differential vulnerability and their characteristic ways of engaging and responding to environments. Reiterating that there is no single optimal environment for development, Wachs (1992) recommends several principles for the design of ecological practice. First, it is important to intervene simultaneously at multiple levels of the environment. Changes in policy, curriculum, and program design at the exosystem level, for instance, must be matched with developmental microsystems. The more environmentally congruent, sustained, and comprehensive the experience, the greater the student change.

Second, practitioners should tailor interventions that capitalize on the student mesosystem, as when programs fit the cultural context in which a student is functioning outside school. This principle validates the need for culturally appropriate interventions, as well as the advantages of family involvement and simultaneous high school and college enrollment.

Third, it is important to accommodate students' varied preferences for microenvironmental niches by offering a variety of activities from which they can choose. Schools and programs that personalize the curriculum around student interests and include experiential opportunities are examples of this student-centered approach to learning activities (Levine, 2002).

Fourth, because not all individuals respond equally well to the same interventions, different kinds of intervention programs are needed. An online financial aid information site might work well for one student, for example, while another student might need personal guidance from a trusted adult. Finally, environmental interventions should build in stress buffers to support students in sustaining their engagement in challenging experiences.

Practitioners have the capacity to influence students' developmentally instigative traits through the provision of people, activities, programs, and tasks that are engaging, responsive, and affirming. Particularly important are experiences of direct instruction, practice, and support for self-management and study habits and skills. Providing different kinds of activities and programs that engage students with varied interests and learning styles (selective responsivity) and tailoring environments that accommodate different preferences for complexity (structuring proclivities) are strategies that work with and develop students' motivational dispositions. Teachers, counselors, and program staff also need to be aware of the directive beliefs of their students and provide opportunities for meaningful achievement and role models that help students believe in their capacity to succeed. Developmental relationships and activities feature a central focus on good proximal processes that engage students in sustained and optimally complex environmental interactions. Close positive relationships with adult teachers, counselors, and mentors have consistently been shown to result in increased student engagement, aspirations, and college outcomes.

Another repeated finding is the importance of a college-going school culture. Efforts to help families understand how to help their children succeed academically and how to negotiate higher education pathways effectively can influence students' family microsystem. College readiness programs can draw on what is known about best cross-environment practices to help students with psychosocial and academic preparation skills, knowledge, and tasks leading to success in college. In particular, having direct interaction with a higher education institution (as opposed to an indirect experience) appears to be highly influential in boosting college readiness. Dual-enrollment programs and early college high school arrangements (Kisker, 2006; Nodine, 2009), connections to college student mentors and tutors (Hayward, Brandes, Kirst, and Mazzeo, 1997), and on-campus visits and activities have all shown strong associations with college success (Bedsworth, Colby, and Doctor, 2006).

Although schools and programs typically concentrate on a subset of relevant tasks, college readiness requires attention to the interactions that occur across a student's mesosystem. "The atomistic nature of most of the intervention strategies is increasingly being recognized as a possible culprit for [the socioeconomic] disparity in college participation rates" (Cabrera and others, 2006, p. 80). For practitioners, the lessons of the mesosystem feature the need for sustained, comprehensive programs and services. The importance of a college-going school culture implies a mesosystem approach in which all of the people and activities in a school immerse students in college readiness activities and consistent messages about the value and achievability of higher education. A typical school or preparation program does not offer everything that students need to be college ready. Realistically, the key to comprehensiveness is through collaborative efforts among schools, colleges, and programs. Working for a seamless, congruent overall environment means making sure all the elements of college readiness are addressed somewhere in the student's mesosystem. It also means identifying discrepant microsystems and devising interventions to minimize their dissonance. School and program staff can also reduce conflict between microsystems through connectors who join and mediate experience across settings (Hayward, Brandes, Kirst, and Mazzeo, 1997). Bringing college into the student's microsystem and maximizing the overlap between people in the community, family, and school are additional strategies for optimal mesosystem interaction.

Finally, the ecological approach implies that successful educational practice requires attention to time: the chronosystem. Progress in achieving college readiness across American youth requires appropriate timing of interventions according to the intersection of student developmental levels and college readiness tasks (Savitz-Romer, 2012). Much more attention is needed to nonstandard trajectories to college, such as those of adult students, GED holders, and delayed and discontinuous college entrants.

Moving Toward an Ecological Approach to College Readiness

The environmental systems lens suggests that the reason that most programs, interventions, and policies fail to improve college readiness lies in their failure to change the ecology of student development. Many of the pieces of a comprehensive, integrated strategy for college readiness are in place. For instance, the importance of the socioeconomic gap in college readiness and the need for K–16 collaboration are widely accepted. College access and success theoretical models have become more complex. Researchers have identified a set of factors that affect student outcomes, and evaluators have specified best practices in college readiness programs. Scores of educational policy initiatives and school reform designs have been introduced for the purpose of assisting low-income students to prepare for, enter, finance, and graduate from college. Despite these promising developments, however, improvement in U.S. college readiness levels has been inhibited by the inability of educators, organizations, and policies to transform the life course of economically and educationally challenged students across the collective contexts and linked time periods of their lives.

We have urged the adoption of an ecological conception of college readiness as the next step for the field. When educators, researchers, and policymakers focus on interconnections between active individuals and multiple environments, they will be positioned to understand the process of college readiness more adequately and intervene more effectively. Having come so far in understanding the individual elements of college readiness, it is time to connect these pieces conceptually and practically. We have suggested, in particular, the importance of research and evaluation models that focus on higher-order interactions and developmental processes. Educational practitioners will be most effective, we argue, when they implement ecological principles by attending to the intersections among students' roles and offering a variety of engaging learning settings that accommodate individual differences and provide a balance of complexity and support. Policymakers must concentrate on the ways that educational reforms and program designs function in the lives of students. K–12 and higher education partnerships and coordinating foundation efforts are particularly promising approaches that follow students over time, intervene through multiple layers of their environment, and encompass K–16 solutions. And issues of time, ideology, and culture need to be understood as affecting research, policy, and educational practice.

In short, accounting for multiple influences, understanding individual differences in environmental susceptibility, and knitting together aspects of students' lives through sustained, comprehensive interventions are the next steps for college readiness research, policy, and practice. Addressing the ecology of college readiness, we believe, can help all stakeholders in our combined efforts to reduce social inequalities in college readiness and enable all students to graduate from high school with the knowledge, skills, and financial resources to enter college and attain a postsecondary degree.

References

ACT. (2011). *The condition of college and career readiness.* Iowa City, IA: ACT.

Adelman, C. (1999). *Answers in the tool box: Academic intensity, attendance patterns and bachelor's degree attainment.* Washington, DC: U.S. Department of Education.

Adelman, C. (2006). *The toolbox revisited: Paths to degree completion from high school through college.* Washington, DC: U.S. Department of Education.

Aldeman, C. (2010). *College- and career-ready: Using outcomes data to hold high schools accountable for student success.* Washington, DC: Education Sector.

Allen, L., and Murphy, L. (2008). *Leveraging postsecondary partners to build a college-going culture: Tools for high school/postsecondary partnerships.* Boston: Jobs for the Future.

American Youth Policy Forum. (1997). *Some things do make a difference for youth.* Washington, DC: Author.

Antrop-Gonzalez, R., and De Jesus, A. (2006). Toward a theory of critical care in urban small school reform: Examining structures and pedagogies of caring in two Latino-community based schools. *International Journal of Qualitative Studies in Education, 19,* 409–433.

Arendale, D. R. (2010). *Access at the crossroads.* ASHE Higher Education Report, *35*(6). San Francisco: Jossey-Bass.

Arnold, K. D., and others. (2009, Fall). The summer flood: The invisible gap among low-income students. *National Education Association Higher Education Journal,* 1–14.

Aud, S., and others. (2010). *The condition of education 2010.* Washington, DC: National Center for Educational Statistics.

Avery, C., and Kane, T. J. (2004). Student perceptions of college opportunities: The Boston COACH program. In C. Hoxby (Ed.), *College decisions: The new economics of choosing, attending and completing college* (pp. 355–394). Chicago: University of Chicago Press.

Bailey, M. J., and Dynarski, S. M. (2011). *Gains and gaps: Changing inequality in U.S. college entry and completion* (NBER working paper, no. 17633). Cambridge, MA: National Bureau of Economic Research.

Bailey, T. R., and Karp, M. M. (2002). *What role can dual enrollment programs play in easing the transition between high school and postsecondary education?* Washington, DC: U.S. Department of Education.

Baker, D. B., Clay, J. N., and Gratama, C. A. (2005). *The essence of college readiness: Implications for students, parents, schools, and researchers.* Mill Creek, WA: Berg Group.

Bandura A. (1997). *Self-efficacy: The exercise of control.* New York: Freeman.

Barnes, W., and Slate, J. R. (2010). College-readiness: The current state of affairs. *Academic Leadership Live, 8*(4), 1–13.

Barnes, W., Slate, J. R., and Rojas-LeBouef, A. (2010). College-readiness and academic preparedness: The same concepts? *Current Issues in Education, 13*(4), 1–28.

Beasley, S. E. (2011). "Country roads take me . . . ? An ethnographic case study of college pathways among rural, first generation students." Unpublished doctoral dissertation, Boston College.

Beasley-Wojick, L., Braggs, C., and Schneider, B. (2011). *Increasing low-socioeconomic status student enrollment in college: Why they don't go—The devil is in the details.* Paper presented at the annual meeting of the Association for the Study of Higher Education, Charlotte, NC.

Bedsworth, W., Colby, S., and Doctor, J. (2006). *Reclaiming the American dream.* San Francisco: Bridgespan Group.

Bell, A. D., Rowan-Kenyon, H. T., and Perna, L. W. (2009). College knowledge of 9th and 11th grade students: Variation by school and state context. *Journal of Higher Education, 80*(6), 663–685.

Benson, P. L., Scales, P. C., Hamilton, S. F., and Sesma, A., Jr. (2006). Positive youth development: Theory, research and applications. In W. Damon and R. M. Lerner (Eds.), *Handbook of child psychology* (6th ed., Vol. 1, pp. 894–941). Hoboken, NJ: Wiley.

Bergerson, A. A. (2009). *College choice and access to college: Moving policies, research and practice to the 21st century.* ASHE Higher Education Report, *35*(2). San Francisco: Jossey-Bass.

Berkner, L., and Chavez, L. (1997). *Access to postsecondary education for 1992 high school graduates.* Washington, DC: National Center for Education Statistics.

Berry, L. (2003). Bridging the gap: A community college and area high schools collaborate to improve student success in college. *Community College Journal of Research and Practice, 27,* 393–407.

Berzin, S. C. (2010). Educational aspirations among low-income youths: Examining multiple conceptual models. *Children and Schools, 32*(2), 112–124.

Blackhurst, A. E., and Augur, R. W. (2008). Precursors to the gender gap in college enrollment: Children's aspirations and expectations for their futures. *Professional School Counseling, 11*(3), 149–158.

Bonous-Hammarth, M., and Allen, W. R. (2005). A dream deferred: The critical factor of timing in college preparation and outreach. In W. G. Tierney, Z. B. Corwin, and J. E. Colyar (Eds.), *Preparing for college: Nine elements of effective outreach* (pp. 155–172). Albany, NY: SUNY Press.

Bourdieu, P. (1967). Systems of education and systems of thought. *International Social Science Journal, 19*(3), 338–358.

Bourdieu, P. (1977). Cultural reproduction and social reproduction. In J. Karabel and A. H. Halsey (Eds.), *Power and ideology in education* (pp. 487–511). New York: Oxford University Press.

Bourdieu, P. (1986). The forms of capital. In J. G. Richardson (Ed.), *Handbook of theory and research in the sociology of education* (pp. 241–258). Westport, CT: Greenwood Press.

Bourdieu, P., and Passeron, J. C. (1977). *Reproduction in education, society, and culture.* Thousand Oaks, CA: Sage.

Bowen, W. G., Chingos, M. M., and McPherson, M. S. (2009). *Crossing the finish line: Completing college at America's public universities.* Princeton, NJ: Princeton University Press.

Brady-Amoon, P., and Fuertes, J. N. (2011). Self-efficacy, self-rated abilities, adjustment, and academic performance. *Journal of Counseling and Development, 89,* 431–438.

Bridgeland, J., and Bruce, M. (2011). *2011 National Survey of School Counselors: Counseling at a crossroads.* New York: College Board.

Broh, B. A. (2002). Linking extracurricular programming to academic achievement: Who benefits and why. *Sociology of Education, 75*(1), 69–91.

Bronfenbrenner, U. (1974). Developmental research, public policy, and the ecology of childhood. *Child Development, 45,* 1–5.

Bronfenbrenner, U. (1979). *The ecology of human development.* Cambridge, MA: Harvard University Press.

Bronfenbrenner, U. (1986). Recent advances in research on the ecology of human development. In R. K. Silbereisen, K. Eyferth, and G. Rudinger (Eds.), *Development as action in context: Problem behavior and normal youth development* (pp. 286–309). New York: Springer-Verlag.

Bronfenbrenner, U. (1993). The ecology of cognitive development: Research models and fugitive findings. In R. H. Wozniak and K. W. Fischer (Eds.), *Development in context: Acting and thinking in specific environments* (pp. 3–44). Mahwah, NJ: Erlbaum.

Bronfenbrenner, U. (1995). Developmental ecology through time and space: A future perspective. In P. Moen, G. H. Elder Jr., and K. Lüscher (Eds.), *Examining lives in context: Perspectives in ecology of human development* (pp. 619–647). Washington, DC: American Psychological Association.

Bronfenbrenner, U. (2001). The bioecological theory of human development. In N. Smelser and P. Baltes (Eds.), *International encyclopedia of the social and behavioral sciences* (Vol. 10, pp. 6963–6970). New York: Elsevier.

Bronfenbrenner, U. (2005). *Making human beings human: Bioecological perspectives on human development.* Thousand Oaks, CA: Sage.

Bronfenbrenner, U., and Ceci, S. J. (1994). Nature-nurture reconceptualized in developmental perspective: A bioecological model. *Psychological Review, 101*(4), 568–586.

Bronfenbrenner, U., and Morris, P. A. (2006). The bioecological model of human development. In R. M. Lerner (Ed.), *Handbook of child psychology* (Vol. 1, pp. 793–828). Hoboken, NJ: Wiley.

Bryan, J., Holcomb-McCoy, C., Moore-Thomas, C., and Day-Vines, N. L. (2009). Who sees the school counselor for college information? A national study. *Professional School Counseling, 12*(4), 1–12.

Cabrera, A. F., and others. (2006). Increasing the college preparedness of at-risk students. *Journal of Latinos and Education, 5*(2), 79–97.

Cabrera, A. F., and La Nasa, S. M. (2000). Understanding the college-choice process. In A. F. Cabrera and S. M. La Nasa (Eds.), *Understanding the college choice of disadvantaged students* (pp. 5–22). San Francisco: Jossey-Bass.

Cabrera, A. F., and La Nasa, S. M. (2001). On the path to college: Three critical tasks facing America's disadvantaged. *Research in Higher Education, 42*(2), 119–149.

Callan, P. M., and others. (2006). *Claiming common ground: State policymaking for improving college readiness and success.* San Jose, CA: National Center for Public Policy and Higher Education.

Castleman, B., Arnold, K. D., and Wartman, K. L. (2012). Stemming the tide of summer melt: An experimental study of the effects of post–high school summer intervention on low-income students' college enrollment. *Journal of Research on Educational Effectiveness, 5*(1), 1–17.

Checkley, K. (2001). Algebra and activism: Removing the shackles of low expectations: A conversation with Robert P. Moses. *Educational Leadership, 59*(2), 6–11.

Cheng, S., and Starks, B. (2002). Racial differences in the effects of significant others on students' educational expectations. *Sociology of Education, 75*(4), 306–327.

Choy, S. (2001). *Students whose parents did not go to college: Postsecondary access, persistence, and attainment.* Washington, DC: National Center for Education Statistics.

Coleman, J. S., and others. (1966). *Equality of educational opportunity.* Washington, DC: Department of Health, Education and Welfare.

Conley, D. T. (2005). *College knowledge: What it really takes for students to succeed and what we can do to get them ready.* San Francisco: Jossey-Bass.

Conley, D. T. (2010). *College and career ready: Helping all students succeed beyond high school.* San Francisco: Jossey-Bass.

Correll, S. J. (2001). Gender and the career choice process: The role of biased self-assessments. *American Journal of Sociology, 106*(6), 1691–1730.

Crosnoe, R. (2000). Friendships in childhood and adolescence: The life course and new directions. *Social Psychology Quarterly, 63*, 377–391.

Crosnoe, R. (2001). Academic orientation and parental involvement in education during high school. *Sociology of Education, 74*(3), 210–230.

Currie, J., and Moretti, E. (2002). *Mother's education and the intergenerational transmission of human capital: Evidence from college openings and longitudinal data.* Cambridge, MA: National Bureau of Education Research.

Dee, T. S. (2005). A teacher like me: Does race, ethnicity, or gender matter? *American Economic Review, 95*(2), 158–165.

Deil-Amen, R., and Turley, R. (2007). A review of the transition to college literature in sociology. *Teachers College Record, 109*, 2324–2366.

Deming, D., and Dynarski, S. (2009). *Into college, out of poverty? Policies to increase the postsecondary attainment of the poor* (NBER working paper, no. 15387). Cambridge, MA: National Bureau of Economic Research.

Dounay, J. (2008). *Strategies to empower low-income and minority students in gaining admission to and paying for college.* Denver, CO: Education Commission of the States.

Druckman, R. (2007). Getting on the college track in fifth grade. In L. G. Dotolo and A. J. Larrance (Eds.), *Access to higher education through consortia.* New Directions for Higher Education, no. 138. San Francisco: Jossey-Bass.

Dweck, C. S. (2000). *Self-theories: Their role in motivation, personality, and development.* Philadelphia: Psychology Press.

Eckes, S. E., and Rapp, K. E. (2006). Charter school research: Trends and implications. In E. P. St. John (Ed.), *Readings on equal education* (Vol. 21, pp. 3–36). Brooklyn, NY: AMS Press.

Eckstein, Z., and Wolpin, K. I. (1999). Why youths drop out of high school: The impact of preferences, opportunities, and abilities. *Econometrica, 67*(6), 1295–1339.

Elder, G. H., and Shanahan, M. J. (2006). The life course and human development. In R. M. Lerner (Ed.), *Handbook of child psychology* (Vol. 1, pp. 665–715). Hoboken, NJ: Wiley.

Engle, J., Bermeo, A., and O'Brien, C. (2006). *Straight from the source: What works for first-generation college students.* Washington, DC: Pell Institute for the Study of Opportunity in Higher Education.

Epstein, J. L. (1990). School and family connections: Theory, research and implications for integrating sociologies of education and family. In D. G. Unger and M. B. Sussman (Eds.), *Families in community settings: Interdisciplinary perspectives* (pp. 99–126). New York: Haworth Press.

Epstein, J. L. (1995). School/family/community partnerships: Caring for the children we share. *Phi Delta Kappan, 76,* 701–712.

Evans, N. J., and others. (2010). *Student development in college: Theory, research, and practice* (2nd ed.). San Francisco: Jossey-Bass.

Fan, X., and Chen, M. (2001). Parental involvement and students' academic achievement: A meta-analysis. *Educational Psychology Review, 13*(1), 1–22.

Fann, A., McClafferty Jarsky, K., and McDonough, P. M. (2009). Parent involvement in the college planning process: A case study of P-20 collaboration. *Journal of Hispanic Higher Education, 8*(4), 374–393.

Fantz, T. D., Siller, T. J., and DeMiranda, M. A. (2011). Pre-collegiate factors influencing the self-efficacy of engineering students. *Journal of Engineering Education, 100*(3), 604–623.

Farmer-Hinton, R. (2010). On being college prep: Examining the implementation of a "college for all" mission in an urban charter school. *Urban Review, 43*(5), 567–596.

Fitch, T., and Marshall, J. L. (2004). What counselors do in high-achieving schools: A study on the role of the school counselor. *Professional School Counseling, 7*(3), 172–177.

Fordham, S., and Ogbu, J. U. (1986). Black students' school success: Coping with the burden of "acting white." *Urban Review, 18,* 176–206.

Friedman, L. (2006). It's never too early: Promoting college prep in middle school after school programs. *Evaluation Exchange, 12*(1), 1–40.

Gambone, M. A., Klem, A. M., and Connell, J. P. (2002). *Finding out what matters for youth: Testing key links in a community action framework for youth development.* Philadelphia: Youth Development Strategies and Institute for Research and Reform in Education.

Gandara, P. (1995). *Over the ivy walls: The educational mobility of low-income Chicanos.* Albany, NY: SUNY Press.

Gandara, P. (2002). A study of high school Puente: What we have learned about preparing Latino youth for postsecondary education. *Educational Policy, 16*(4), 474–495.

Gandara, P. (2004). Building bridges to college. *Educational Leadership, 62*(3), 56–60.

Gandara, P., and Bial, D. (2001). *Paving the way to postsecondary education.* Washington, DC: National Center for Education Statistics.

Gandara, P., Gutierrez, D., and O'Hara, S. (2001). Planning for the future in rural and urban high schools. *Journal of Education for Students Placed at Risk, 6*(1), 73–93.

Gandara, P., and Mejorado, M. (2005). Putting your money where your mouth is: Mentoring as a strategy to increase access to higher education. In W. G. Tierney, Z. B. Corwin, and J. E. Colyar (Eds.), *Preparing for college: Nine elements of effective outreach* (pp. 89–110). Albany, NY: SUNY Press.

Garvey, J., and Grobe, T. (2011). *From GED to college degree: Creating pathways to postsecondary success for high school dropouts.* Jobs for the Future Report. Boston, MA.: Jobs for the Future.

Gelber, S. (2007). Pathways in the past: Historical perspectives on access to higher education. *Teachers College Record, 109*(10), 2252–2286.

Gettinger, M., and Seibert, J. K. (2002). Contributions of study skills to academic competence. *School Psychology Review, 31,* 350–365.

Gibbons, M. M., and Borders, L. D. (2010). A measure of college-going self-efficacy for middle school students. *Professional School Counseling, 13*(4), 234–243.

Goldrick-Rab, S., Carter, D. F., and Wagner, R. W. (2007). What higher education has to say about the transition to college. *Teachers College Record, 109*(10), 2444–2481.

Goldrick-Rab, S., and Han, S. W. (2011). Accounting for socioeconomic differences in delaying the transition to college. *Review of Higher Education, 34*(3), 423–445.

Guest, A., and Schneider, B. (2003). Adolescents' extracurricular participation in context: The mediating effects of schools, communities, and identity. *Child Development, 56,* 415–428.

Gullatt, Y., and Jan, W. (2003). *How do pre-collegiate academic outreach programs impact college-going among underrepresented students?* Boston: Pathways to College Network Clearinghouse.

Hallett, R., and Venegas, K. M. (2011). Is increased access enough? Advanced Placement courses, quality, and success in low-income urban schools. *Journal for the Education of the Gifted, 34*(3), 468–487.

Hammick, M., Freeth, D., Copperman, J., and Goodsman, D. (2009). *Being interprofessional.* Cambridge, UK: Polity Press.

Haskins, R., and Kemple, J. (2009). *A new goal for America's high schools: College preparation for all.* Princeton, NJ: Brookings Institution Policy Brief.

Haycock, K. (2006). *Promises abandoned: How policy choices and institutional practices restrict college opportunities.* Washington, DC: Education Trust.

Hayward, G. C., Brandes, B. G., Kirst, M. W., and Mazzeo, C. (1997). *Higher education outreach programs: A synthesis of evaluations.* Berkeley, CA: Policy Analysis for California Education.

Hearn, J. C. (1984). The relative roles of academic, ascribed, and socioeconomic characteristics in college destinations. *Sociology of Education, 57*(1), 22–30.

Hearn, J. C., and Holdsworth, J. M. (2005). Cocurricular activities and students' college prospects: Is there a connection? In W. G. Tierney, Z. B. Corwin, and J. E. Colyar (Eds.), *Preparing for college: Nine elements of effective outreach* (pp. 135–154). Albany, NY: SUNY Press.

Herlihy, C. (2007). State and district-level support for successful transitions into high school. In L. Kennelly and M. Monrad (Eds.), *Easing the transition to high school: Research and best practices designed to support high school learning* (pp. 17–30). Washington, DC: National High School Center.

Hill, L. D. (2008). School strategies and the "college-linking" process: Reconsidering the effects of high schools on college enrollment. *Sociology of Education, 81*(1), 53–76.

Hill, N. E., and others. (2004). Parent academic involvement as related to school behavior, achievement, and aspirations: Demographic variations across adolescence. *Child Development, 75*(5), 1491–1509.

Hodgkinson, H. (1999). *All one system: A second look.* Washington, DC: Institute for Educational Leadership, National Center for Public Policy and Higher Education.

Hoffman, N., and Vargas, J. (2010). *A policymaker's guide to early college designs: Expanding a strategy for achieving college readiness for all.* Boston: Jobs for the Future.

Holcomb-McCoy, C. (2010). Involving low-income parents and parents of color in college readiness activities: An exploratory study. *Professional School Counseling, 14*(1), 115–124.

Hoover, J. J., and Patton, P. R. (1995). *Teaching students with learning problems to use study skills: A teacher's guide.* Austin, TX: Pro-Ed.

Hossler, D., and Gallagher, K. (1987). Studying student college choice: A three-phase model and the implications for policymakers. *College and University, 62,* 207–221.

Hossler, D., Braxton, J., and Coopersmith, G. (1989). Understanding student college choice. In J. Smart (Ed.), *Higher education: Handbook of theory and research* (Vol. 5, pp. 231–288). New York: Agathon Press.

Hossler, D., Schmit, J., and Vesper, N. (1999). *Going to college: How social, economic, and educational factors influence the decisions students make.* Baltimore, MD: Johns Hopkins University Press.

Hoxby, C. M. (2004). *Achievement in charter schools and regular schools in the United States: Understanding the differences.* Cambridge, MA: Harvard University and National Bureau of Education Research.

Immerwahr, J. (2003). *With diploma in hand: Hispanic high school seniors talk about their future.* San Jose, CA: Public Agenda, National Center for Public Policy and Higher Education.

Irvine, J. J. (1986). Teacher-student interactions: Effects of student race, sex, and grade level. *Journal of Educational Psychology, 7*(1), 14–21.

Iverson, S. V. (2012). Constructing outsiders: The discursive framing of access in university diversity policies. *Higher Education, 35*(2), 149–177.

Jeynes, W. H. (2003). A meta-analysis: The effects of parental involvement on minority children's academic achievement. *Education and Urban Society, 35*(2), 202–218.

Jun, A., and Colyar, J. (2002). Parental guidance suggested: Family involvement in college preparation programs. In W. G. Tierney and L. S. Hagedorn (Eds.), *Increasing access in college: Extending possibilities for all students* (pp. 195–215). Albany, NY: SUNY Press.

Jun, A., and Tierney, W. G. (1999, Spring). At-risk students and college success: A framework for effective preparation. *Metropolitan Universities,* 49–60.

Karabel, J. (2005). *The chosen: The hidden history of admission and exclusion at Harvard, Yale, and Princeton.* Boston: Houghton Mifflin.

Kazis, R. (2006). *Articulation, alignment and the challenge of college-readiness: Testimony to the commission on the future of higher education.* Boston: Jobs for the Future.

Kazis, R., Pennington, H., and Conklin, K. (2003). *Ready for tomorrow: Helping all students achieve secondary and postsecondary success: A guide for governors.* Washington, DC: National Governors Association.

Kemple, J. J. (2004). *Career academies impacts on labor market outcomes and educational attainment.* New York: MDRC.

Kemple, J. J., and Snipes, J. C. (2000). *Career academies: Impacts on students' engagement and performance in high school.* New York: MDRC.

Kemple, J. J., and Willner, C. J. (2008). Career academies: Long-term impacts on labor market outcomes, educational attainment, and transitions to adulthood. New York: MDRC.

Kennelly, L., and Monrad, M. (2007). *Easing the transition to high school: Research and best practices designed to support high school learning.* Washington, DC: National School Center.

Kim, D., and Rury, J. L. (2007). The changing profile of college access: The Truman Commission and enrollment patterns in the postwar era. *History of Education Quarterly, 47*(3), 302–327.

Kimura-Walsh, E., Yamamura, E. K., Griffin, K. A., and Allen, W. R. (2009). Achieving the college dream? *Journal of Hispanic Higher Education, 8*(3), 298–315.

Kisker, C. B. (2006). Integrating high school and the community college: Previous efforts and current possibilities. *Community College Review, 34*(1), 68–86.

Knapp, L. G., Kelly-Reid, J. E., and Ginder, S. A. (2010). *Enrollment in postsecondary institutions, fall 2008; graduation rates, 2002 and 2005 cohorts; and financial statistics, fiscal year 2008.* Washington, DC: National Center for Education Statistics.

Knight-Diop, M. G. (2010). Closing the gap: Enacting care and facilitating black students' educational access in the creation of a high school college-going culture. *Journal of Education for Students Placed at Risk, 15*(1–2), 158–172.

Koyama, J. P. (2007). Approaching and attending college: Anthropological and ethnographic accounts. *Teachers College Record, 109*(10), 2301–2323.

Lammers, W., Onwuegbuzie, A. J., and Slate, J. R. (2001). Academic success as a function of the sex, class, age, study habits, and employment of college students. *Research in the Schools, 8*(2), 71–81.

Le, C., and Frankfort, J. (2011). *Accelerating college readiness: Lessons from North Carolina's innovator early colleges.* Boston: Jobs for the Future.

Lenhart, A., Purcell, K., Smith, A., and Zickuhr, K. (2010). *Social media and mobile Internet use among teens and young adults.* Washington, DC: Pew Internet and American Life Project.

Lerner, R. M. (2006). Developmental science, developmental systems, and contemporary theories of human development. In R. M. Lerner (Ed.), *Handbook of Child Psychology* (Vol. 1, pp. 1–17). Hoboken, NJ: Wiley.

Levine, E. (2002). *One kid at a time: Big lessons from a small school.* New York: Teachers College Press.

Lieberman, J. E. (Ed.). (1988). *Collaborating with high schools.* New Directions for Community Colleges, no. 63. San Francisco: Jossey-Bass.

Lin, N. (2001). *Social capital: A theory of social structure and action.* Cambridge: Cambridge University Press.

Long, B. T. (2007). The contributions of economics to the study of college access and success. *Teachers College Record, 109*(10), 2367–2443.

Long, M. C., Iatarola, P., and Conger, D. (2009). Explaining gaps in readiness for college-level math: The role of high school courses. *American Education Finance Association, 4*(1), 1–33.

Louie, V. (2007). Who makes the transition to college? Why we should care, what we know, and what we need to do. *Teachers College Record, 109*(10), 2222–2251.

Lozano, A., Watt, K. M., and Huerta, J. (2009). A comparison study of 12th grade Hispanic students' college anticipations, aspirations, and college preparatory measures. *American Secondary Education, 38*(1), 92–110.

Lumina Foundation. (2008). *Results and reflections: An evaluation report.* Indianapolis, IN: Lumina Foundation.

Lumina Foundation. (2009). *Making the numbers add up: A guide for using data in college access and success programs.* Indianapolis, IN: Lumina Foundation.

Mars, M. M., Slaughter, S., and Rhoades, G. (2008). The state-sponsored student entrepreneur. *The Journal of Higher Education, 79*(6), 638–670.

Martinez, M., and Klopott, S. (2005). *The link between high school reform and college access and success for low-income and minority youth.* Washington, DC: American Youth Policy Forum and Pathways to College Network.

Mattern, K. D., and Shaw, E. J. (2010). A look beyond cognitive predictors of academic success: Understanding the relationship between academic self-beliefs and outcomes. *Journal of College Student Development, 51*(6), 665–678.

Mazzeo, C. (2010). *College prep for all? What we've learned from Chicago's efforts.* Chicago: Consortium on Chicago School Research.

McCarthy, M. M., and Kuh, G. D. (2006). Are students ready for college? What student engagement data say. *Phi Delta Kappan, 87,* 664–669.

McClafferty, K. A., and McDonough, P. M. (2000). *Creating a K–16 environment: Reflections on the process of establishing a college culture in secondary schools.* Paper presented at the annual meeting of the Association for the Study of Higher Education, Sacramento, CA.

McCormick, N. J., and Lucas, M. S. (2011). Exploring mathematics college readiness in the United States. *Current Issues in Education, 14*(1). Retrieved October 12, 2012, from http://cie.asu.edu/ojs/index.php/cieatasu/article/view/680.

McDonough, P. M. (1997). *Choosing colleges: How social class and schools structure opportunity.* Albany, NY: SUNY Press.

McDonough, P. M., and Calderone, S. (2006). The meaning of money: Perceptual differences between college counselors and low-income families about college costs and financial aid. *American Behavioral Scientist, 49*(12), 1703–1718.

McElroy, E. J., and Armesto, M. (1998). TRIO and Upward Bound: History, programs, and issues—past, present, and future. *Journal of Negro Education, 67*(4), 373–380.

McGrath, D. J., Swisher, R. R., Elder, G.H.J., and Conger, R. D. (2001). Breaking new ground: Diverse routes to college in rural America. *Rural Psychology, 66*(2), 244–267.

McNamee, S. J., and Miller, R.K., Jr. (2009). *The meritocracy myth* (2nd ed.). Lanham, MD: Rowman and Littlefield.

Metcalf, K. K., and Paul, K. M. (2006). Enhancing or destroying equity? An examination of educational vouchers. In E. P. St. John (Ed.), *Readings on equal education* (Vol. 21, pp. 37–78). Brooklyn, NY: AMS Press.

MetLife. (2011). *Survey of the American teacher: Preparing students for college and careers.* New York: Author.

Militello, M., and others. (2009). Identifying exemplary school counseling practices in nationally recognized high schools. *Journal of School Counseling, 7*(13), 1–26.

Mitchell, K., and others. (2005). *Rigor, relevance, and results: The quality of teacher assignments and student work in new and conventional high schools.* Washington, DC: National Evaluation of High School Transformation.

Moen, P., Elder, G.H.J., Glen H. J., and Lüscher, K. (Eds.). (1995). *Examining lives in context: Perspectives on the ecology of human development.* Washington. DC: American Psychological Association.

Moreno, J. F. (2002). The long-term outcomes of Puente. *Educational Policy, 16*(4), 572–587.

Myers, S. M., and Myers, C. B. (2012). Are discussions about college between parents and their high school children a college planning activity? Making the case and testing the predictors. *American Journal of Education, 118*(3), 281–308.

National Center for Education Statistics (2012). Remediation and degree completion. In *The Condition of Education 2012.* NECES #2012045. Washington, DC: Department of Education.

National Research Council. (2002). *Learning and understanding: Improving advanced study of mathematics and science in U.S. high schools.* Washington DC: National Academy Press.

Nodine, T. (2009). *Innovations in college readiness: How early college schools are preparing students underrepresented in higher education for college success.* Boston: Jobs for the Future.

Nodine, T. (2010). *College success for all: How the Hidalgo Independent School District is adopting early college as a district-wide strategy.* Boston: Jobs for the Future.

Obama, B. (2009). *Address to joint session of Congress.* Retrieved May 30, 2009, from http://www.whitehouse.gov/the_press_office/Remarks-of-President-Barack- Obama-Address-to-Joint-Session-of-Congress/.

Oesterreich, H. (2000). *The technical, cultural, and political factors in college preparation programs for urban and minority youth.* New York: ERIC Clearinghouse on Urban Education.

Ogbu, J. (1978). *Minority education and caste: The American system in cross-cultural perspective.* Orlando, FL: Academic Press.

Padilla, R. V. (2009a). The preoccupation with student outcomes. In R. V. Padilla (Ed.), *Student success modeling: Elementary school to college* (pp. 1–21). Sterling, VA: Stylus Publishing.

Padilla, R. V. (2009b). Searching for theory and method. In R. V. Padilla (Ed.), *Student success modeling: Elementary school to college* (pp. 21–46). Sterling, VA: Stylus Publishing.

Pajares, F. (2006). Self-efficacy during childhood and adolescence: Implications for teachers and parents. In F. Pajares and T. Urdan (Eds.), *Self-efficacy beliefs of adolescents* (pp. 71–96). Greenwich, CT: Information Age Publishing.

Pascarella, E. T., Pierson, C. T., Wolniak, G. C., and Terenzini, P. T. (2004). First-generation college students: Additional evidence on college experiences and outcomes. *Journal of Higher Education, 75*(3), 249–284.

Pasque, P. A. (2007). Seeing more of the educational inequities around us: Visions toward strengthening relationships between higher education and society. In E. P. St. John and P. K. Stillman (Eds.), *Readings on equal education* (Vol. 22, pp. 37–84). Brooklyn, NY: AMS Press.

Pathways to College Network. (2002). *Capturing the college potential of students from underserved populations: An analysis of efforts to overcome social and financial barriers to college.* Washington, DC: Author.

Pennington, H. (2004). *Fast track to college: Increasing postsecondary success for all students.* Washington, DC: Center for American Progress and Institute for America's Future.

Pennington, H. (2012, April 8). For student success, stop debating and start improving. *Chronicle of Higher Education.* Retrieved October 24, 2012, from http://chronicle.com/article/For-Student-Success-Stop/131451.

Pennington, H., and Vargas, J. (2004). *Bridge to postsecondary success: High schools in the knowledge economy.* Boston: Jobs for the Future.

Perna, L. W. (2005). The key to college access: Rigorous academic preparation. In W. G. Tierney, Z. B. Corwin, and J. Colyar (Eds.), *Preparing for college: Nine elements of effective outreach* (pp. 113–134). Albany, NY: SUNY Press.

Perna, L. W. (2006). Studying college access and choice: A proposed conceptual model. *Higher Education: Handbook of Theory and Research, 21,* 99–157.

Perna, L. W. (2007). The sources of racial-ethnic group differences in college enrollment: A critical examination. In F. K. Stage (Ed.), *Using Quantitative Data to Answer Critical Questions.* New Directions for Institutional Research, no. 133. San Francisco: Jossey-Bass.

Perna, L. W. (Ed.). (2010). *Understanding the working college student: New research and its implications for policy and practice.* Sterling, VA: Stylus.

Perna, L. W., Fenske, R. H., and Swail, W. S. (2000). Sponsors of early intervention programs. *The ERIC Review, 8*(1), 15–18.

Perna, L. W., and others. (2011). *The potential role of the International Baccalaureate (IB) diploma programme in improving academic preparation for college for all students.* Paper presented at Annual Meeting of the Association for the Study of Higher Education, Charlotte, NC.

Perna, L. W., Rowan-Kenyon, H. T., Thomas, S. L., and Bell, A. (2008). The role of college counseling in shaping college opportunity: Variations across high schools. *Review of Higher Education, 31*(2), 131–159.

Perna, L. W., and Swail, W. S. (2001). Pre-college outreach and early intervention. *Thought and Action, 17*(1), 99–110.

Perna, L. W., and Thomas, S. L. (2008). *A conceptual model for understanding disciplinary approaches to student success.* ASHE Higher Education Report, *34*(1). San Francisco: Jossey-Bass.

Perna, L. W., and Titus, M. A. (2004). Understanding differences in the choice of college attended: The role of state public policies. *Review of Higher Education, 27*(4), 501–525.

Piaget, J. (1970). *Genetic epistemology.* (E. Duckworth, Trans.). New York: Columbia University Press.

Portes, P. R. (1999). Social and psychological factors in the academic achievement of children of immigrants: A cultural history puzzle. *American Educational Research Journal, 36*(3), 489–507.

Priest, D. M., St. John, E. P., and Boon, R. D. (2006). Introduction. In D. M. Priest and E. P. St. John (Eds.), *Privatization and public universities* (pp. 1–10). Bloomington: Indiana University Press.

Quint, J. (2001). *Scaling up first things first: Site selection and the planning year.* New York: Manpower Demonstration Research Corp.

Quint, J., Thompson, S. L., and Bald, M. (2008). *Relationships, rigor and readiness. Strategies for improving high schools.* New York: MDRC.

Ramsey, J., and Gorgol, L. (2010). *Expanding access and opportunity: The Washington State Achievers program.* Washington, DC: Institute for Higher Education Policy.

Raywid, M. A. (1998). Small schools: A reform that works. *Educational Leadership, 55*(4), 34–37.

Reardon, S. F. (2011). The widening academic achievement gap between the rich and the poor: New evidence and possible explanations. In G. Duncan and R. J. Murnane (Eds.), *Wither opportunity: Rising inequality, schools, and children's life chances* (pp. 91–116). New York: Russell Sage Foundation.

Rendon, L. I. (2002). Community college Puente: A validating model of education. *Educational Policy, 16*(4), 642–667.

Renn, K. A., and Arnold, K. D. (2003). Reconceptualizing research on college student peer culture. *Journal of Higher Education, 74*(3), 261–291.

Resnick, L. B. (1983). Mathematics and science learning: A new conception. *Science, 220,* 477–478.

Robbins, S. B., and others. (2004). Do psychosocial and study skill factors predict college outcomes? A meta-analysis. *Psychological Bulletin, 130*(2), 261–288.

Robbins, S. B., and others. (2006). Unraveling the differential effects of motivational and skills, social, and self-management measures from traditional predictors of college outcomes. *Journal of Educational Psychology, 98*(3), 598–616.

Roderick, M., Nagaoka, J., and Coca, V. (2009). College readiness for all: The challenge for urban high schools. *Future of College, 19*(1), 185–210.

Roderick, M., Nagaoka, J., Coca, V., and Moeller, E. (2008). *From high school to the future: Potholes on the road to college.* Chicago: Consortium on Chicago School Research.

Rosenbaum, J. E. (2011). The complexities of college for all: Beyond fairy-tale dreams. *Sociology of Education, 84*(2), 113–117.

Rowan-Kenyon, H. T., Bell, A. D., and Perna, L. W. (2008). Contextual influences on parental involvement in college going: Variations by socioeconomic class. *Journal of Higher Education, 79*(5), 564–586.

Rueda, R. (2005). Making sense of what we know: From nine propositions to future research
and interventions. In W. G. Tierney, Z. B. Corwin, and J. E. Colyar (Eds.), *Preparing for
college: Nine elements of effective outreach* (pp. 189–200). Albany, NY: SUNY Press.

Rueda, R., Monzó, L. D., and Arzubiaga, A. (2003, September 16). Academic instrumental
knowledge: Deconstructing cultural capital theory for strategic intervention approaches.
Current Issues in Education, 6(14). Retrieved October 1, 2012, from http://cie.asu.edu/
volume6/number14/.

Savitz-Romer, M. (2012). The gap between influence and efficacy: College readiness training,
urban school counselors, and the promotion of equity. *Counselor Education and Supervision,
51,* 98–111.

Savitz-Romer, M., and Bouffard, S. M. (2012). Reading, willing, and able: A developmental
approach to college access and success. Cambridge, MA: Harvard University Press.

Schultz, J. L., and Mueller, D. (2006). *Effectiveness of programs to improve postsecondary education enrollment and success of underrepresented youth.* St. Paul, MN: Wilder Research.

Scott, T. P., Tolson, H., and Lee, Y. H. (2010). Assessment of Advanced Placement participation and university academic success in the first semester: Controlling for selected high
school academic abilities. *Journal of College Admission, 208,* 26–30.

Sedlacek, W. E. (2004). *Beyond the big test: Noncognitive assessment in higher education.* San
Francisco: Jossey-Bass.

Seftor, N. S., Mamun, A., and Schirm, A. (2009). *The impacts of regular Upward Bound on postsecondary outcomes 7-9 years after scheduled high school graduation.* Princeton, NJ: Mathematica.

Shear, L., and others. (2005). *Creating cultures for learning: Supportive relationships in new and
redesigned high schools.* Menlo Park, CA: SRI International.

Shulock, N. (2010). *Beyond the rhetoric: Improving college readiness through coherent state policy.*
Washington, DC: National Center for Public Policy and Higher Education.

Skinner, E. A., and Belmont, M. J. (1993). Motivation in the classroom: Reciprocal effects of
teacher behavior and engagement across the school year. *Journal of Educational Psychology,
85*(4), 571–581.

Slaughter, S., and Leslie, L. L. (1999). *Academic capitalism: Politics, policies, and the entrepreneurial university.* Baltimore, MD: Johns Hopkins University Press.

Slaughter, S., and Rhoades, G. (2004). *Academic capitalism and the new economy: Markets, state,
and higher education.* Baltimore, MD: Johns Hopkins University Press.

Smith, M. J. (2008). College choice process of first generation black female students: Encouraged to what end? *Negro Educational Review, 59*(3–4), 147–162.

Snipes, J. C., Holton, G. I., Doolittle, F., and Sztejnberg, L. (2006). *Striving for student success:
The effect of Project GRAD on high school student outcomes in three urban school districts.* New
York: MDRC.

Sokatch, A. (2006). Peer influences on the college-going decisions of low socioeconomic status
urban youth. *Education and Urban Society, 39*(1), 128–146.

Solorzano, D. G., and Villalpando, O. (1998). Critical race theory, marginality, and
the experiences of students of color in higher education. In C. A. Torres and T. R.
Mitchell (Eds.), *Sociology of education: Emerging perspectives* (pp. 299–319). Albany, NY:
SUNY Press.

Spencer, M. B. (2006). Phenomenology and ecological systems theory: Development of diverse groups. In R. M. Lerner (Ed.), *Handbook of child psychology* (Vol. 1, pp. 829–893). Hoboken, NJ: Wiley.

St. John, E. P. (1991). What really influences minority attendance? Sequential analyses of the High School and Beyond sophomore cohort. *Research in Higher Education, 32*(2), 141–158.

St. John, E. P. (Ed.). (2004). *Readings on equal education.* Brooklyn, NY: AMS Press.

St. John, E. P. (2006). *Education and the public interest: School reform, public finance, and access to higher education.* New York: Springer.

St. John, E. P. (Ed.). (2007). *Confronting educational inequality: Reframing, building understanding, and making change.* Brooklyn, NY: AMS Press.

St. John, E. P., Cabrera, A. F., Nora, A., and Asker, E. H. (2001). Economic perspectives on student persistence. In J. Braxton (Ed.), *Rethinking the departure puzzle: New theory and research on college student retention.* Nashville, TN: Vanderbilt University Press.

Stanton-Salazar, R. D. (2004). Social capital among working-class minority students. In M. A. Gibson, P. Gándara, and J. P. Koyama (Eds.), *School connections: U.S. Mexican youth, peers, and school achievement.* New York: Teachers College Press.

Stanton-Salazar, R. D. (2011). A social capital framework for the study of institutional agents and their role in the empowerment of low-status students and youth. *Youth and Society, 43*(3), 1066–1109.

Steele, C. M., and Aronson, J. (1995). Stereotype threat and the intellectual test performance of African-Americans. *Journal of Personality and Social Psychology, 62*(1), 26–37.

Steinberg, A., and Allen, L. (2011). Putting off-track youths back on track to college. *Phi Delta Kappan, 92*(2), 21–26.

Steinberg, A., Almeida, C., Allen, L., and Goldberger, S. (2003). *Four building blocks for a system of educational opportunity: Developing pathways to and through college for urban youth.* Boston: Jobs for the Future.

Steinberg, L., Darling, N. E., and Fletcher, A. C. (1995). Authoritative parenting and adolescent adjustment: An ecological journey. In P. Moen, G. H. Elder Jr., and K. Lüscher (Eds.), *Examining lives in context: Perspectives on the ecology of human development* (pp. 423–466). Washington, D.C.: American Psychological Association.

Steinberg, L., Dornbusch, S. M., and Brown, B. (1992). Ethnic differences in adolescent achievement: An ecological perspective. *American Psychologist, 47*(6), 723–729.

Super, C. M., and Harkness, S. (2002). Culture structures the environment for development. *Human Development, 45*(4), 270–274.

Super, D. E. (1990). A life-span, life-space approach to career development. In D. Brown and L. Brooks (Eds.), *Career choice and development: Applying contemporary approaches to practice* (pp. 11–20). San Francisco: Jossey-Bass.

Swail, W. S. (Ed.). (2000). *Preparing America's disadvantaged for college: Programs that increase college opportunity.* New Directions for Institutional Research, no. 107. San Francisco: Jossey-Bass.

Swail, W. S. (2004). *Value added: The costs and benefits of college preparatory programs.* Washington, DC: Education Policy Institute.

Swail, W. S., and Perna, L. W. (2000). A view of the landscape: Results of the national survey of outreach programs. In *Outreach program handbook 2001* (pp. xvii–xxxvi). New York: College Board.

Swail, W. S., and Perna, L. W. (2002). Pre-college outreach and early intervention programs: A national imperative. In W. G. Tierney and L. S. Hagedorn (Eds.), *Increasing access to college: Extending the possibilities for all students* (pp. 15–34). Albany, NY: SUNY Press.

Swail, W. S., and Roth, D. (2000). The role of early intervention in education reform. *ERIC Review, 8*(1), 13–18.

Symonds, W. C., Schwartz, R. B., and Ferguson, R. (2011). *Pathways to prosperity: Meeting the challenge of preparing young Americans for the 21st century.* Report issued by the Pathways to Prosperity Project. Cambridge, MA: Harvard Graduate School of Education.

Tafel, J., and Eberhart, N. (1999). *Statewide school-college (K–16) partnerships to improve student performance.* Denver, CO: State Higher Education Executive Officers.

Thayer, P. B. (2000, May). Retention of students from first generation and low income backgrounds. *Opportunity Outlook,* 2–8.

Thelen, E., and Smith, L. B. (2006). Dynamic systems theories. In R. M. Lerner (Ed.), *Handbook of child psychology* (Vol. 1, pp. 258–312). Hoboken, NJ: Wiley.

Thomas, L., and Quinn, J. (2007). *First generation entry into higher education.* Maidenhead, England: Society for Research into Higher Education and Open University Press.

Tienda, M., and others. (2003). *Closing the gap? Admissions and enrollments at the Texas public flagships before and after affirmative action.* Princeton, NJ: Texas Higher Education Opportunity Project.

Tierney, W. G. (2004). Academic triage: Challenges confronting college preparation programs. *Qualitative inquiry, 10,* 950–962.

Tierney, W. G., and Auerbach, S. (2005). Toward developing an untapped resource: The role of families in college preparation. In W. G. Tierney, Z. B. Corwin, and J. E. Colyar (Eds.), *Preparing for college: Nine elements of effective outreach* (pp. 29–48). Albany, NY: SUNY Press.

Tierney, W. G., and Colyar, J. E. (2005). The role of peer groups in college preparation programs. In W. G. Tierney, Z. B. Corwin, and J. E. Colyar (Eds.), *Preparing for college: Nine elements of effective outreach* (pp. 49–68). Albany, NY: SUNY Press.

Tierney, W. G., and Garcia, L. D. (2008). Preparing underprepared students for college: Remedial education and early assessment programs. *Journal of At-Risk Issues, 14*(2), 1–7.

Tierney, W. G., and Garcia, L. D. (2011). Remediation in higher education: The role of information. *American Behavioral Scientist, 55*(2), 102–120.

Tierney, W. G., and Hagedorn, L. S. (2007). *Making the grade in college prep: A guide for improving college preparation programs.* Los Angeles: Center for Higher Education Policy Analysis, University of Southern California.

Tierney, W. G., and Jun, A. (2001). A university helps prepare low income youths for college: Tracking school success. *Journal of Higher Education, 72*(2), 205–225.

Tierney, W. G., and Venegas, K. (2007). The cultural ecology of financial aid decision making. In E. P. St. John and P. K. Stillman (Eds.), *Readings on equal education* (Vol. 22, pp. 1–37). Brooklyn, NY: AMS Press.

Tierney, W. G., and Venegas, K. M. (2009). Finding money on the table: Information, financial aid, and access to college. *Journal of Higher Education, 80*(4), 363–388.

Tornatzky, L., Cutler, R., and Lee, J. (2002). *College knowledge: What Latino parents need to know and why.* Claremont, CA: Tomas Rivera Policy Institute.

Tournaki, N. (2003). Effect of student characteristics on teachers' predictions of student success. *Journal of Educational Research, 96*(5), 310–319.

Trybus, M. A., and Li, R. (1998, April). *Effects of a partnership academy on school and career success of at-risk high school students.* Paper presented at the annual meeting of the American Educational Research Association, San Diego, CA. (ED 423 593)

U.S. Department of Education. (2003). *College preparation checklist.* Washington, DC: U.S. Government Printing Office.

U.S. Department of Education. (2006). *A test of leadership: Charting the future of U.S. higher education.* Washington, DC: U.S. Government Printing Office.

Van Buskirk, W., and McGrath, D. (1999). *The ACE advantage: Charting the pathway from high school to college.* New York: National Center for Urban Partnerships.

van Merrienboer, J.J.G., and Ayres, P. (2005). Research on cognitive load theory and its design implications for e-learning. *Educational Technology Research and Design, 53*(3), 5–13.

Vargas, J. H., and Miller, M. S. (2011). Early college designs. *School Administrator, 68*(6), 18–25.

Venezia, A., and Kirst, M. W. (2005). Inequitable opportunities: How current education systems and policies undermine the chances for student persistence and success in college. *Educational Policy, 19*(2), 283–307.

Venezia, A., Kirst, M. W., and Antonio, A. (2002). *Betraying the college dream: How disconnected K–12 and postsecondary education systems undermine student aspirations.* Palo Alto, CA: Stanford University Bridge Project.

Villalpando, O., and Solorzano, D. G. (2005). The role of culture in college preparation programs: A review of the research literature. In W. G. Tierney, Z. B. Corwin, and J. E. Colyar (Eds.), *Preparing for college: Nine elements of effective outreach* (pp. 13–28). Albany, NY: SUNY Press.

Vitale, D., and Schmeiser, C. B. (2006). What the ACT reveals about reading readiness. *Community College Journal, 76*(6), 20–23.

Wachs, T. D. (1992). *The nature of nurture: Individual differences and development series* (3rd ed.). Thousand Oaks, CA: Sage.

Walpole, M. (2003). Socioeconomic status and college: How SES affects college experiences and outcomes. *Review of Higher Education, 1*(27), 45–73.

Walpole, M. (2007). *Economically and educationally challenged students in higher education: Access to outcomes.* ASHE Higher Education Report, *33*(3). San Francisco: Jossey-Bass.

Walsh, E. J. (2004). P-16 policy alignment in the states: Findings from a 50-state survey. *States Schools and Colleges Policies to Improve Student Readiness for College and Strengthen Coordination Between Schools and Colleges,* 23–34. Retrieved October 25, 2012, from http://www.highereducation.org/reports/ssc/index.shtml.

Warburton, E. C., Bugarin, R., Nuñez, A.-M., and Carroll, C. D. (2001). *Bridging the gap: Academic preparation and postsecondary success of first-generation students.* Washington, DC: National Center for Education Statistics.

Wartman, K. L., and Savage, M. (2008). *Parental involvement in higher education.* ASHE Higher Education Report, *33*(6). San Francisco: Jossey-Bass.

Wasley, P. A., and others. (2000). *Small schools, great strides: A study of new small schools in Chicago.* New York: Bank Street College of Education.

Watt, K. M., Huerta, J., and Lozano, A. (2007). A comparison study of AVID and GEAR UP 10th-grade students in two high schools in the Rio Grande Valley of Texas. *Journal of Education for Students Placed at Risk, 2*(2), 185–212.

Wechsler, H. S. (2001). *Access to success in the urban high school: The middle college movement.* New York: Teachers College Press.

Wimberley, G. L., and Noeth, R. J. (2005). *College readiness begins in middle school: ACT policy report.* Iowa City, IA: ACT.

Winkle-Wagner, R. (2010). *Foundations of educational inequality: Cultural capital and social reproduction.* ASHE Higher Education Report, *36*(1). San Francisco: Jossey-Bass.

Winkleby, M. A., and others. (2009). Increasing diversity in science and health professions: A 21-year longitudinal study documenting college and career success. *Journal of Science Education and Technology, 18*(6), 535–545.

Yamamura, E. K., Martinez, M. A., and Saenz, V. B. (2010). Moving beyond high school expectations: Examining stakeholders' responsibility for increasing Latina/o students' college readiness. *High School Journal, 93*(3), 126–148.

Zafft, C., Kallenbach, S., and Spohn, J. (2006). *Transitioning adults to college: Adult basic education program models.* Cambridge, MA: National Center for the Study of Adult Learning and Literacy.

Zelkowski, J. (2010). Secondary mathematics: Four credits, block schedules, continuous enrollment? What maximizes college readiness? *Mathematics Educator, 20*(1), 8–21.

Zhang, J. (2010). *From GED credential to college: Patterns of participation in postsecondary education programs.* Washington, DC: American Council on Education.

Zimmerman, B. J. (1998). Academic studying and the development of personal skill: A self-regulatory perspective. *Educational Psychologist, 33*, 73–86.

Name Index

A

Adelman, C., 27, 32, 34, 35, 85
Alderman, C., 78
Allen, L., 54, 55, 56, 60, 64, 86
Allen, W. R., 31, 35, 45, 84, 88
Almeida, C., 60, 64,
Antonio, A., 50
Antrop-Gonzalez, R., 39
Arendale, D. R., 4
Armesto, M., 63
Arnold, K. D., 8, 25, 42, 47, 60, 86, 88, 89
Aronson, J.; 13
Arzubiaga, A., 52
Asker, E. H., 26
Aud, S., 1
Auerbach, S., 43, 49, 50, 51
Augur, R. W., 27
Avery, C., 24
Ayres, P., 22

B

Bailey, M. J., 1, 4, 84
Bailey, T. R., 66
Baker, D. B., 4
Bald, M., 34, 39
Bandura, A., 25
Barnes, W., 2, 84
Beasley, S. E., 80
Beasley-Wojick, L., 53
Bedsworth, W., 50, 53, 85, 105
Bell, A. D., 32, 39, 40, 44, 49, 51
Belmont, M. J., 28

Benson, P. L., 40
Bergerson, A. A., 53, 99
Berkner, L., 24
Bermeo, A., 42
Berry, L., 34
Berzin, S. C., 27, 89
Bial, D., 42, 51, 87
Blackhurst, A. E., 27
Bonous-Hammarth, M., 84, 88
Boon, R. D., 78
Borders, L. D., 87
Bouffard, S. M., 88
Bourdieu, P., 48
Bowen, W. G., 1, 4
Brady-Amoon, P., 26
Braggs, C., 53
Brandes, B. G., 42, 52, 53, 61, 86, 88, 91, 100, 105
Bridgeland, J., 51
Broh, B. A., 45
Bronfenbrenner, U., 7, 8, 11, 12, 13, 14, 15, 17, 18, 19, 20, 21, 25, 28, 29, 31, 59, 83
Brown, B., 45
Bruce, M., 51
Bryan, J., 40
Bugarin, R., 36

C

Cabrera, A. F., 17, 19, 24, 26, 43, 85, 87, 91, 105
Calderone, S., 24
Callan, P. M., 69

Mejorado, M., 53
Metcalf, K. K., 68
Militello, M., 34, 39, 40, 51
Miller, M. S., 56
Miller, R. K., Jr., 77
Mitchell, K., 32
Moeller, E., 24
Moen, P., 8, 11
Monrad, M., 87, 88
Monzó, L. D., 52
Moore-Thomas, C., 40
Moreno, J. F., 52, 53
Moretti, E., 84
Morris, P. A., 8, 11, 12, 14, 20, 83
Mueller, D., 41, 42, 100
Murphy, L., 55, 56
Myers, C. B., 51
Myers, S. M., 51

N

Nagaoka, J., 24, 60
Nodine, T., 34, 37, 56, 67, 105
Noeth, R. J., 45, 50, 51, 87
Nora, A., 26
Nuñez, A.-M., 36

O

Obama, B., 4
O'Brien, C., 42
Oesterreich, H., 49, 51, 52
Ogbu, J. U., 45
O'Hara, S., 88
Onwuegbuzie, A. J., 23

P

Padilla, R. V., 2, 4, 7–8, 11, 14, 31, 46, 91
Pajares, F., 26
Pascarella, E. T., 27
Pasque, P. A., 61, 79, 81, 97
Passeron, J. C., 48
Patton, P. R., 23
Paul, K. M., 68
Pennington, H., 60, 61, 67, 69, 78, 81, 86
Perna, L. W., 2, 3, 4, 6, 7, 19, 20, 31, 32,
    39, 40, 41, 44, 45, 49, 51, 53, 60, 61,
    62, 66, 85, 87, 89, 91, 100

Piaget, J., 22
Pierson, C. T., 27
Portes, P. R., 4, 79
Priest, D. M., 78
Purcell, K., 45

Q

Quinn, J., 2
Quint, J., 34, 39, 70

R

Ramsey, J., 65, 73
Rapp, K. E., 68
Raywid, M. A., 65
Reardon, S. F., 4, 5, 35, 79, 84
Rendon, L. I., 53
Renn, K. A., 8, 60
Resnick, L. B., 22
Rhoades, G., 78
Robbins, S. B., 20, 23, 26
Roderick, M., 24, 60
Rojas-LeBouef, A., 2
Rosenbaum, J. E., 78
Roth, D., 63
Rowan-Kenyon, H. T., 32, 39, 40,
    44, 49, 51
Rueda, R., 19, 20, 40, 46, 51, 52
Rury, J. L., 83

S

Saenz, V. B., 43, 45
St. John, E. P., 4, 26, 27, 62, 63, 64, 67,
    70, 72, 78, 79, 80, 81, 84
Savage, M., 50
Savitz-Romer, M., 40, 88, 106
Scales, P. C., 40
Schirm, A., 41, 54
Schmeiser, C. B., 89
Schmit, J., 24, 44, 72
Schneider, B., 45, 53
Schultz, J. L., 41, 42, 100
Schwartz, R. B., 78
Scott, T. P., 53
Sedlacek, W. E., 26
Seftor, N. S., 41, 54
Seibert, J. K., 23, 29

Subject Index

A

Academic habits: description of, 23; as resource characteristic of college readiness, 23; study skills, 23

Academic preparation: career focus of, 38; college readiness and, 22; college-going culture of, 37; course work providing, 32–35; gap between K–12 and college, 3; microsystem of, 32–40; pedagogy impact on, 35–37; school counselor role in, 39–40; small learning environments for, 38–39; teacher-student relationships and, 39

Academic preparation microsystem: career focus element of, 38; college-going culture element of, 37; course work element of, 32–35; description of, 32; pedagogy element in, 35–37; school counselors element of, 39–40; small learning environments element of, 38–39; teacher-student relationships element of, 39

Academic self-discipline, 23

ACE Plus, 66

Achieve, 71

Achieving a College Education (ACE), 66

ACT: data from test takers of, 23; requiring high school students to take, 34

Advanced Placement (AP) courses, 34–35, 53, 65–66

Advancement Via Individual Determination (AVID), 41, 43, 52, 70

African Americans. *See* Black students

American's Choice programs, 70

Asian Americans students: college knowledge by, 25; high school course taking and college success connection for, 34–35. *See also* Racial/ethnic differences

Aspirations college readiness: description of, 27; low-income and at-risk students and diminishing, 89; as socially constructed, 27. *See also* Motivation

AVID (Advancement Via Individual Determination), 41, 43, 52, 70

B

Baltimore College Bound, 43

Basic Education Opportunity Grant, 71

Big Picture Learning high schools, 38

Bill and Melinda Gates Foundation, 55, 61, 67, 73, 81, 103

Black students: college knowledge by, 25; high school course taking and college success connection for, 32; less peer-based support of achievement by, 45; positive effects of college-going culture for, 37; as vulnerable to stereotype threat, 13. *See also* Racial/ethnic differences

Boston Public School seniors study, 24–25

Bronfenbrenner's ecological theory of human development: environmental contexts of, 14–17; environmental interactions in, 17–18; exosystem as discussed in, 59–60; introduction to, 8–9, 11–12

C

Career academies, 38, 65
Career development theory, 38
Career focus, 38
Chronicle of Higher Education (Pennington commentary), 81
Chronosystem level: description of, 83; development change in the, 88–89; ecological context of, 89; same-age cohorts connecting macrosystem and, 83–84; sequence and timing of college readiness, 84–88; timing and duration of interventions as being within the, 87
City University of New York, 66
Claiming Common Ground report, 69
Coalition of Essential Schools, 70
Cocurricular activities, 45
College access: economic models of rational choice on, 80; macrosystem level view on, 78, 79
College Board, 62, 87
College knowledge: description of, 24; how socioeconomic status and parental experience impacts, 24–25, 43–44; lower levels of Latino, 25, 44; racial/ethnic differences in, 25
College Now, 66
"College Preparation Checklist" (U.S. Department of Education), 85
College preparation programs: confirming college enrollment and academic preparedness relationship, 27; description and some examples of, 41, 43; effective practices in outreach and, 42; evaluation and research literature on, 41, 43; inclusion of culture in, 48–49
College readiness: broader construct of, 3; chronosystem level of, 83–89; complexity of, 4–6; definition of, 1–2; exosystem level of, 59–75; growing institutional interest in, 2–3; interactions and relationships as

causality in, 17–18, 19; key elements of, 20*fig*; macrosystem level of, 16–17, 77–82, 83–84; mesosystem level of, 47–57; microsystem level of, 31–46; overview of human ecology framework of, 11–18, 94–98; "pathway" or "pipeline" metaphor of, 17, 84, 86–87; proximal processes for changes in, 14; quasi-ecological approaches to, 6–8; School reform designed to promote, 61–62, 64–68; state and federal initiatives designed to help with, 68–69; strategies to develop in school contexts, 33*t*–34*t*. *See also* Ecological model of college readiness; Student development
College readiness indicators: aspirations as, 27, 89; demand characteristics, 21, 27–28; developmentally instigative characteristics or, 19–20; force characteristics, 21, 25–27; Free Application for Federal Study Aid filled out during high school as, 86; resource characteristics, 20–25
College readiness programs: design as part of student exosystem, 60–61; as focus of research, policy, and practice, 3
College readiness research: using ecological approach in evaluation and, 98–101; focus of, 3–4; implications for policy, 101–103; implications for practice, 103–106; looking to the next generation of, 8; moving toward an ecological approach to, 106–107; overview of human ecology framework for, 11–18, 94–98
College student tutors, 54
College-going culture, 37
College-high school integration, 53–56
Completion rates, 2
Comprehensive School Reform (CSR), 70
Council of Chief State School Officers, 71
Course work: academic preparation through, 32, 34–35; Advanced Placement (AP), 34–35, 53, 65–66; connection of reduced completion rates to remedial, 2; International

Baccalaureate courses, 53, 65–66; rigorous and college-level courses offered in high school, 65–66. *See also* Pedagogy

Creating a College Culture project, 37

Cultural capital: educational stratification explained through, 47–48; mesosystem interactions context of, 48–49

Culture: college preparation program addressing issue of, 48–49; ecological context of ideology and, 81–82; high school's college-going, 37; macrosystem level enshrined in language making ideology and, 79–81

D

Demand characteristics: description of, 21; how college readiness is facilitated by, 27–28

Developmental systems models, 8

Dual-credit or dual-enrollment programs, 54, 66–67

E

Early college and middle college high schools, 55, 56, 67

Early College High School (ECHS) program, 67

Early College High School Initiative, 55, 56

Ecological model of college readiness: Bronfenbrenner's ecological theory of human development, 8–9, 11–12, 14–17; chronosystem level of, 83–89; environmental contexts of, 14–17; exosystem level of the, 59–75; illustrated diagram of, 92*fig*; implications for policy, 101–103; implications for practice, 103–106; macrosystem level of the, 16–17, 77–82, 83–84; mesosystem level of the, 47–57; microsystem level of the, 31–46; moving toward the adoption of, 106–107; need for future research on, 91; principles of development in, 11–13; process-person-person-context-time (PPCT) theory on, 8, 11, 13,

14–17, 93; using in research and evaluation, 98–101; summarizing current research on, 90–94. *See also* College readiness; Environment-person interactions

Economic models of rational choice, 80

Education Trust, 63

Educational attainment: family socioeconomic status and subsequent, 25, 43–44; relationship between college costs and, 72–73

Enrollment management practice, 72

Environment (small learning), 38–39

Environment-person interactions: as causality of college readiness, 17–18, 19; chronosystem level of, 83–89; ecological context of, 29; exosystem of the, 59–75; human ecology framework contexts of, 14–17; macrosystem level of the, 16–17, 77–82, 83–84; mesosystem network of overlapping relationships and, 47–57; microsystem of direct student, 31–46; reciprocal nature of, 13; self-efficacy as product of, 26; student development through experiences in their "immediate," 13; summarizing current research on, 90–94. *See also* Ecological model of college readiness; Students

EQUITY 2000, 66

Ethnicity. *See* Racial/ethnic differences

Exosystem level: Bronfenbrenner's ecological theory on, 59–60; college readiness program design as part of students,' 60–61; description of, 59; federal government role in, 70–73; foundations and nonprofit organizations role in, 73–74; of leaders and policymakers attempting to reform curriculum, 61–62; literature describing organization and policy, 60; precollege intervention programs as, 62–64; restructuring of K–12 curriculum as, 60; school reform as, 61–62, 64–68; state and federal initiatives role in, 68–69; systems and structures in, 74–75

F

Facebook college applications, 45

Families: academic achievement and support and encouragement of, 43–44; change due to development and accompanying environmental change, 88–89; children's subsequent education level and socioeconomic status of, 25, 43–44; college knowledge related to parental experience, 24–25; parental role in student's social capital, 49–50; social media aids to college preparation by, 46

Family educational involvement, 49–51, 88–89

Family engagement, 49–50

Federal government: common curriculum standards development by, 70–71; financing higher education role by, 71–73; initiatives to promote college readiness, 68–69; school reform role played by, 70

Financial aid: Basic Education Opportunity Grant on, 71; as critical factor influencing student success, 75; enrollment management practice for, 72; federal government role in, 71–73; Free Application for Federal Study Aid, 86; increasing academic achievement focus of, 64; Pell Grant program for, 54, 71–72; political and legislative movements reaching students through, 84; study findings on lack of Upward Bound effect on, 54; study on students' lack of understanding of, 75; Talent Search providing information on, 62–63. *See also* Higher education; Low-income students; Students

First Things First, 70

Force characteristics: aspirations as, 27; description of, 21, 25; self-efficacy as, 25–26

Fordham Foundation, 71

Foundations: Bill and Melinda Gates Foundation, 55, 61, 67, 73, 81; exosystem level role of, 73–74; Fordham Foundation, 71; Lumina Foundation, 61. *See also* Nonprofit Organizations

Free Application for Federal Study Aid, 86

G

Gaining Early Awareness and Readiness for Undergraduate Programs (Gear UP), 41, 43, 63, 87

Gates Foundation, 55, 61, 67, 73, 81

GEAR UP program, 41, 43, 63, 87

H

"Helicopter parents," 50

High school: academic preparation through course work of, 32–35; career focus by, 38; cocurricular activities during, 45; college readiness programs used to bridge gap between college and, 3; college-going culture fostered during, 37; conception of time and future possibilities during, 88; declining parental involvement from middle to, 49–51, 88–89; mesosystem integration of college and, 53–56; school counselors of, 39–40, 52; teacher-student relationships impact on, 39. *See also* K–12 education

High school. *See* K-12 education

Higher education: "college for all" view of macrosystem level of, 78, 79; college readiness programs used to bridge gap between K-12 and, 3; commercialization of, 78; relationship between college costs and attainment of, 72–73. *See also* Financial aid

Higher Education Act, 63

Human capital theory, 80

I

Ideology: ecological context of culture and, 81–82; language and subculture of, 79–81; macrosystem level and foundational, 77–79; theory as carrier of, 80

Immigration patterns, college readiness impacted by, 4

Indiana 21st Century Scholars Program, 87

Inigral's Schools App., 45–46

Instructional styles: characteristics of successful, 37; impacting academic knowledge and skills, 36–37. *See also* Teachers

International Baccalaureate program, 53, 65–66

Internet: academic preparation and college knowledge through, 45; Web-based college readiness applications through the, 45–46

J

Jobs for the Future (JFF), 67, 69

Johns Hopkins Center for Research on the Education of Students Placed at Risk, 74

K

K–12 education: college readiness programs used to bridge gap between college and, 3; establishing common standards for curriculum of, 70–71; exosystem of curriculum structuring of, 60; school reform of, 61–62, 64–68; school-to-college programs focused on alignment of, 61, 69, 87. *See also* High school

L

Language of ideology, 79–81

Latino students: high school course taking and college success connection for, 32; less peer-based support of achievement by, 45; lower levels of college knowledge of, 25, 44; positive effects of college-going culture for, 37. *See also* Racial/ethnic differences

"Leaky education pipeline," 69

Low-income students: diminishing college aspirations over time, 89; enrollment management practice's negative effect on, 72; lack of orderly sequence to college readiness by, 86; lack of parental involvement with education of, 49–51,

88–89; Pell Grant program for, 54, 71–72; relationship between college costs and educational attainment by, 72–73. *See also* Financial aid; Students

Lumina Foundation, 61

M

Macrosystem level: changing nature of, 16–17; "college for all" view of the, 78, 79; description of, 77; ecological context of culture and ideology of, 81–82; foundational beliefs and ideology that make up the, 77–79; language, subculture, and theory of, 79–81; same-age cohorts connecting chronosystem and, 83–84; underlying the U.S. social structure, 77–79

MESA (Mathematics, Engineering, and Science Achievement), 41

Mesosystem level: college and high school integration of, 53–56; cultural capital and the, 47–49; description of the, 47; overlapping relationships in ecological context of, 56–57; social capital and connectors of, 49–53

Microsystem level: academic preparation in schools, 32–40; description of, 31; direct study experience in an ecological context, 46; literature on college preparation, 31–32; out-of-school, 40–46

Motivation: low-income students and diminishing, 89; self-discipline is tied closely to, 23. *See also* Aspirations college readiness

N

National Alliance of Business and Education Trust, 71

National Assessment of Educational Progress High School Transcript Study (2005), 35

National Board of Governors, 71

National Center for Education Statistics (NCES), 2, 54

National Center for Public Policy and Higher Education, 69

School choice programs, 67

School counselors: mesosystem connector role of, 52; student microsystem role of, 39–40

School reform: categories of, 64–68; college readiness in K–12 schools form of, 64; diverse leaders and policies of, 61–62

School reform categories: Advanced Placement (AP) courses, 34–35, 53, 65–66; career academies, 38, 65; dual-credit or dual-enrollment programs, 54, 66–67; early college and middle college high schools, 55, 56, 67; International Baccalaureate course, 53, 65–66; rigorous and college-level courses offered in high school, 65–66; school choice programs, 67; small schools, 65

Self-appraisal (or self-rated ability), 26

Self-efficacy: description of, 25; as force characteristic of college readiness, 25–26; self-appraisal (or self-rated ability) aspect of, 26

Small learning environments, 38–39

Small schools programs, 65

Social capital: mesosystem connectors and, 49–53; role of parents in student, 49–50

Social media: academic preparation and college knowledge through, 45; Web-based college readiness applications through, 45–46

Social structure: connections between educational outcomes and, 81–82; language, subculture, and theory supporting, 79–81; macrosystem level support of existing, 16–17, 77–82

Standards for K-12 curriculum, 70–71

State college readiness initiatives, 68–69

State Higher Education Executive Officers, 63

Status attainment theory, 80

Student development: chronosystem level of, 88–89; defined in context of ecological systems, 11–12; ecological framework of, 12*fig*; macrosystem level of the, 16–17; "pathway" or "pipeline" metaphor of increasing college readiness in, 17, 84, 86–87. *See also* College readiness

Student Support Services, 62, 63

Students: college readiness indicators of, 19–29; college tutor positions of, 54; conception of time and future possibilities of, 88; demand characteristics of, 21, 27–28; educators' instructional practices influenced by race of, 28; enrollment management practice's negative effect on low-income, 72; force characteristics of, 21, 25–27; resource characteristics of, 20–25; study on lack of financial aid understanding by, 75; teachers' treatment based on demographic characteristics of, 28. *See also* Environment-person interactions; Financial aid; Low-income students

Study skills, 23

T

Talent Development High Schools (TDHS) model, 36, 74

Talent Search, 62

Teachers: instructional practices influenced by student race, 28; treatment of students based on demographic characteristics, 28. *See also* Instructional styles

Teacher-student relationship: high school academic preparation and, 39; racial and demographic factors impacting, 28

"Transition to college" research, 91

TRIO programs, 62–63

Two-year colleges, 54

U

University of Southern California, 54

University Park Campus School (Worcester, MA), 36

Upward Bound, 41, 54, 62

Urban Systemic Initiative, 66

U.S. Department of Education, 4, 70, 85

W

Washington State Achievers Program, 73, 75

About the Authors

Karen D. Arnold, Ph.D., is associate professor of higher education at Boston College. She is the author of books and articles in the fields of college access, talent development, and longitudinal study methods. She directs the Big Picture Longitudinal Study of low-income high school graduates. Arnold has been vice president for student services at Reed College, visiting fellow at the Murray Research Center for the Study of Lives at Radcliffe College, and visiting scholar at the Oxford Centre for Higher Education Policy Studies at the University of Oxford.

Elissa C. Lu is a Ph.D. candidate at Boston College and an institutional research analyst at Harvard University. Over the past ten years, she has led dozens of educational research and evaluation projects through her work at Eduventures, a higher education research and consulting firm, and the Museum of Science in Boston. She has also taught and mentored low-income adults and youth for several years, most recently in an adult education bridge-to-college program. Her research focuses on affordability, access, and student debt.

Kelli J. Armstrong is the vice president of institutional research, planning, and assessment at Boston College and has worked in institutional research at both public and private institutions, including Tufts University and the Massachusetts Board of Higher Education, and as a director for the University of Massachusetts system. Her background in enrollment management includes her work as an assistant dean of admissions at Bates College and associate vice chancellor for enrollment management at the University of Massachusetts Boston, where she managed programs to provide college access for students from low-income backgrounds.

About the ASHE Higher Education Report Series

Since 1983, the ASHE (formerly ASHE-ERIC) Higher Education Report Series has been providing researchers, scholars, and practitioners with timely and substantive information on the critical issues facing higher education. Each monograph presents a definitive analysis of a higher education problem or issue, based on a thorough synthesis of significant literature and institutional experiences. Topics range from planning to diversity and multiculturalism, to performance indicators, to curricular innovations. The mission of the Series is to link the best of higher education research and practice to inform decision making and policy. The reports connect conventional wisdom with research and are designed to help busy individuals keep up with the higher education literature. Authors are scholars and practitioners in the academic community. Each report includes an executive summary, review of the pertinent literature, descriptions of effective educational practices, and a summary of key issues to keep in mind to improve educational policies and practice.

The Series is one of the most peer reviewed in higher education. A National Advisory Board made up of ASHE members reviews proposals. A National Review Board of ASHE scholars and practitioners reviews completed manuscripts. Six monographs are published each year and they are approximately 144 pages in length. The reports are widely disseminated through Jossey-Bass and John Wiley & Sons, and they are available online to subscribing institutions through Wiley Online Library (http://wileyonlinelibrary.com).

Call for Proposals

The ASHE Higher Education Report Series is actively looking for proposals. We encourage you to contact one of the editors, Dr. Kelly Ward (kaward@wsu.edu) or Dr. Lisa Wolf-Wendel (lwolf@ku.edu), with your ideas.

Recent Titles

ORDER FORM SUBSCRIPTION AND SINGLE ISSUES

DISCOUNTED BACK ISSUES:

Use this form to receive 20% off all back issues of *ASHE Higher Education Report.*
All single issues priced at **$23.20** (normally $29.00)

TITLE	ISSUE NO.	ISBN

Call 888-378-2537 or see mailing instructions below. When calling, mention the promotional code JBNND to receive your discount. For a complete list of issues, please visit www.josseybass.com/go/aehe

SUBSCRIPTIONS: (1 YEAR, 6 ISSUES)

☐ New Order ☐ Renewal

U.S.	☐ Individual: $174	☐ Institutional: $307
CANADA/MEXICO	☐ Individual: $174	☐ Institutional: $367
ALL OTHERS	☐ Individual: $210	☐ Institutional: $418

Call 888-378-2537 or see mailing and pricing instructions below.
Online subscriptions are available at www.onlinelibrary.wiley.com

ORDER TOTALS:

Issue / Subscription Amount: $ _____

Shipping Amount: $ _____
(for single issues only – subscription prices include shipping)

Total Amount: $ _____

SHIPPING CHARGES:	
First Item	$6.00
Each Add'l Item	$2.00

(No sales tax for U.S. subscriptions. Canadian residents, add GST for subscription orders. Individual rate subscriptions must be paid by personal check or credit card. Individual rate subscriptions may not be resold as library copies.)

BILLING & SHIPPING INFORMATION:

☐ **PAYMENT ENCLOSED:** *(U.S. check or money order only. All payments must be in U.S. dollars.)*

☐ **CREDIT CARD:** ☐ VISA ☐ MC ☐ AMEX

Card number _____ Exp. Date _____

Card Holder Name _____ Card Issue # _____

Signature _____ Day Phone _____

☐ **BILL ME:** *(U.S. institutional orders only. Purchase order required.)*

Purchase order # _____
Federal Tax ID 13559302 • GST 89102-8052

Name _____

Address_____

Phone_____ E-mail_____

Copy or detach page and send to: **John Wiley & Sons, One Montgomery Street, Suite 1200, San Francisco, CA 94104-4594**

Order Form can also be faxed to: **888-481-2665**

PROMO JBNND

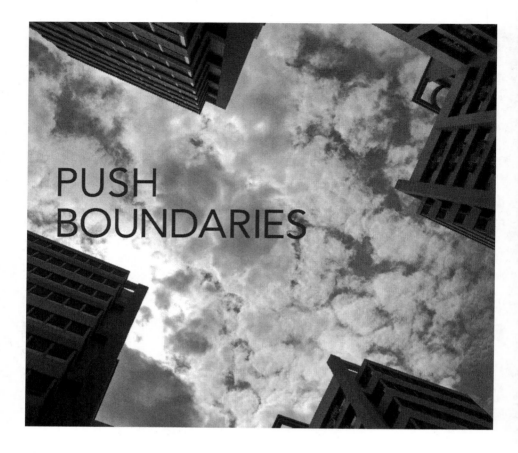